THE K.
OF
THE FLAME

An Introduction To The Spirit of Philosophy

by

D. J. Ciraulo

Athena Lithographie

Previously published by Association for Philosophy and Education, 1986

ISBN-13: 978-1511623032
ISBN-10: 1511623039

To my mother who instilled in me a desire for education...
and the memory of my father, who showed me the meaning of the earth.

Table of Contents

EDITOR'S PREFACE

It is quite by accident that at a time when there exists a great deal of commotion about the meaning of education—a time when technological advances appear to be moving in direct inverse proportion to qualitative thought—curious, that at this time I should happen upon an anonymous collection of papers which, in their own way, strike at the heart of the issue. And the issue is best expressed by Heidegger's statement:

> *"Most thought provoking in a thought provoking time is that we are still not thinking."*[1]

But how can this be? How can this great thinker say we are not thinking when we are inundated with bits of information, blocks of statistical studies, and have solved so many interesting problems? Is it simply because we have not, and possibly cannot "process" all this data? And is it indeed a fact that human understanding can be, or even should be, modeled on an input-output problem solving process? Perhaps we should be more concerned with the differences between information retrieval and wisdom, or with the important distinction between being "smart" and becoming "intelligent." Why, for instance, do we prefer to organize our thoughts in terms of mechanics, quantification and verifiability, instead of being a bit more concerned with what is vitalistic, qualitative and authentic? And when we do attempt to create something of qualitative value —something which may affect our internal lives,— why do we do so by way of "how to" handbooks? Why, since Galileo, do we continue to equate thinking "only" with the ability to control and manipulate things? Have we exhausted our thought about an object when

---

1.   Cf. Heidegger, What is Called Thinking

its movement has been calculated and its essence categorized and brought under our domination? Or, is there something here, which remains unthought? But ironically this line of questioning is precisely the kind of fundamental thinking to which we have turned a deaf ear and blind eye. Why is this so?

Are these kinds of questions—philosophical questions—too impractical to be of concern, or do they touch in an uncomfortable way that which lies closest to heart? And why do we continue to try and cure the issue in question by prescribing more of the same medicine—more information, more data, more studies? Do we really think that statistics and logistics can bring about the change of heart and mind necessary for an enlightened and just civilization, or, are we now in danger of using these tools to mask a profound thoughtlessness?

We are certainly born with the capacity to walk, talk, and think, but not with a guarantee for their completion and perfection. Although it has traditionally been the task of education to help refine, bring forth, and actualize these potentialities, this ideal has recently been abandoned in favor of the far easier task of teaching specific techniques and newly found "methods" and "means" which help us to attain "ends" which remain unjustified. But as we obtain our just rewards and accumulate more "know how," we are falling into deeper despair—a kind of despair which remains suspiciously unaware of itself, but is, never the less, expressed in the numbness, passivity, and the outbreaks of violence symptomatic of a whole generation. And how is it that at a time when access to information and "computer literacy" is at an all time high, and climbing, the international educational rankings of our country are precipitously falling? Is it possible that we have learned certain modes of thinking without proper concern for what desperately needs to be thought? What needs to be thought, according to Heidegger, is the nature of thinking and its relation to what is thought-provoking. How, then, are we to learn this way of thinking?—and to whom should we turn?

As with all true learning, we will naturally turn to those who have mastered their particular art; and only one branch of knowledge has taken on the task of thinking about the nature of thought itself—this is philosophy! When Plato was asked about philosophical thinking, he replied:

> "[Philosophy] does not admit of exposition like other branches of knowledge; but after much converse about the matter itself and a life lived together suddenly a light, as it were, is kindled in one soul by a flame that leaps to it from another, and thereafter sustains itself."[2]

So before we proceed to the study of philosophy, which is the art of thinking about that which always remains to be thought, we should understand that it cannot be reduced to a mere technique intended to accomplish a set task, but must, like all art forms, first be inspired and desired for its own sake.

These simple and unassuming papers do not deal with a philosophy, nor do they present and solve the problems of philosophy; what they do represent is an attempt on the part of a teacher to draw his students into the realm where thinking is most thoughtful—and into the "spirit of philosophy."

II

Before I acquaint the reader with the chain of events that brought these notes and letters to my attention, I would first like to ask the reader a question. The question I would like to ask concerns the nature of a question itself. What is a question? And have you ever really experienced one? I say experienced, because all true learning and thinking is predicated upon a vital question—not one you merely ask, but one you

2.   Cf. Plato, The Seventh Letter

live through. Such questions are not abstract, that is, they are not asked in order to predict something, elicit a right or wrong answer, nor calculated to gain information, or prove what one has already decided upon; they are put forth in order to open up a new region in which "to be" and "think." With vital questions, "thinking" and "being" are the same! And these kinds of questions can only be asked if we ourselves are first put in question, that is, if we ourselves have become questionable in our very being. To become questionable in one's being means to lose the rut and track that guides our everyday actions and grounds our existence. Only when we become ungrounded and unsure of our own position, can we become ready for the possibility of learning something else, that is, of not only seeing another point of view, but also becoming something else. This being-ready-for and turning-towards that which is to be learned makes possible the space of dialogue in which thinking and learning take place.

A vital question requires a vital answer, and so must always be asked in the context of dialogue. And this is so even if the interlocutor—as in the famous case of Socrates—is one's own inner voice (*daimonion*) It is in dialogue that we risk our position by confronting an alternate way to think and be. It is always through the silent gaze of the other that our own thinking and being is brought into question. In monologue we risk nothing; the questions we ask are abstract and calculated to conform to our own assumptions. When we confront an object as to its weight, color or composition, the answers we receive have nothing to do with who or what we are. Things do not answer back! They do not cause us to reflect upon ourselves. All too often we face each other in monologue, where from behind our well-armed bulwark of prejudice, presupposition, and hearsay, we shoot our arrows of factual information at the defended fortress of the other. A monologue assumes that all has been learned—that there is nothing left to say! But a vital question—a question on which our lives depend—must by its nature remain problematic. In this way the question stays in keeping with the growth and becoming of life itself by staying responsive and on the move. The concept of "justice," for instance, must continually be brought into question and kept alive by each of us in each successive and changing generation. Vital questions—those concerning what Whitehead called "matters of importance" (not merely "matters of fact," but what tells us what to do with the facts or how to evaluate them)—find their proper place in the open-ended space of dialogue, which of its nature always presents another point of view. This will insure that the notion of "justice" does not calcify into a dead concept. A living answer is gained in struggle and must forever remain questionable and open to the changes and unforeseen dangers which life presents.

III

It is often in the midst of what is most ordinary and commonplace that an event may take place, which brings us face to face with something, quite interesting and unusual. What is curious about such an occurrence is the unpredictable and innocuous way it happens. It was on an occasion such as this that these papers were brought to my attention: a student approached me one morning and asked if I would look at something he had found. He removed from his binder a loosely collected assortment of pages, which were brown with age and partially eaten away. He informed me that he was helping to clear away an orchard when he happened upon the papers. I later found out that it was an old ranch—the last of its kind in the valley; it was a place with a large stately home at its center, surrounded by rows of withered trunks and leafless branches. But more important to our story was the dilapidated cottage situated in a grove of elms at the periphery of the property. It was a weatherworn shack that leaned down toward the banks of a dried-up creek. It appears that while the young man was tearing out a large plank from the walls of the cottage, a bundle of papers fell to the floor from an adjoining old bookshelf. As he quickly leafed through them, he noticed the word *philosophy* written on one of the pages, and so decided to bring them to class. After a cursory glance at what seemed to be a group of letters and lecture notes, I informed my student that there was nothing I could see of value in the papers ...but that I should, nevertheless, like to take a second look at them. Secretly, I became immediately intrigued by the unusual circumstances surrounding their discovery.

What I subsequently found were not arbitrary notes, but a series of questions and answers, which were probably recorded in order to be organized in the future. I later found out from a grandson of the original property owner that the seasonal workers in the orchard occupied the shack in the past. But the letters and notes were more than trivial or discontinuous but were written in such a way as to put into simple language the meaning and experience of philosophy. I have since organized the questions and answers into a finished dialogue form, and have embellished certain parts only where necessary. I have, of course, not touched the letters, but simply arranged them chronologically. The author was obviously a man who was familiar with the history of ideas, and a lover of education and teaching. But why were these papers left in this manner? The grandson could only tell me that as a boy playing in his grandfathers orchard, he remembered an older Italian man who would return every summer to work and supervise the younger workers; and that at the time, the grandson said, he didn't understand the name they lightly, but respectfully, called the old man: Maestro. It now seems apparent from what I have gathered from the marginal notes and implications of his last letter that the Maestro was most likely forced, probably in the early thirties, to leave his homeland—to be exiled not only from his people and his natural language, but also from his true vocation.

And so it is that our author came to this land where he followed the seasons from place to place and put his hands to work in pruning back the trees of our orchards; but I am sure that whenever he could, whether at noonday or when work was done at twilight, he would engage the younger newly immigrated workers in conversation and slowly draw them into a region where thinking is most thoughtful and young minds most fully flourish.

Well, this is how I came to be in possession of, or better, how I was possessed and claimed by these papers. But who was our wandering author? Where was he from? And where else did he possibly work? Are there, perhaps, more papers which might be added to his more serious work? The reader is, of course, incredulous about all this! Why, you ask, should anyone care? How could something of any worth be buried away? These are indeed good questions. But I cannot help being concerned and disheartened when I see the bounty of so many orchards plowed under, and so many flames flicker for a while and fade.

Acknowledgements

I would like to thank my two daughters Dina and Darlene for their support and unconditional love. I am especially grateful to Paula Swanson for her help with the manuscript and time spent on corrections. And to professors Drago Šiljak and A. Dipippo,—who both encouraged me to rework the project—I offer my gratitude and respect.

A DIALOGUE:

ON GODS, MEN AND WILD GAME

Part One

Scene: *It is a warm spring day and in the midst of a large orchard an old man is busily pruning back the branches of an apricot tree. Two young men approach and call to him.*

Paolo: Look! He waves his shears at the top of ladder as though he were conducting Verdi—a little more from this branch, a little less from that one—now 'fortissimo'!

                               The young men applaud.

Alessandro: Bravo! Maestro, come down. We have red, cool wine from the cellars and bread and cheese.

Paolo: Yes, your performance can wait.

                               From the midst of the trees the old man turns, happy to see his two young friends.

Maestro: I must say, you've come not a bit too soon—look how the sun rides high in the sky. Let's sit here in the shade this tree provides and give thanks to...

Alessandro: I know... to the gods. We must pour libations to the gods... as we usually do.

Paolo: Must we always waste wine?

Alessandro: Maestro, pay no attention to Paolo. What prayer will you compose for us today?

                               Undaunted, the old man solemnly

20

stands, jug in hand, and as he pours red wine on the orchard floor he declares:

Maestro:　Let us pour libations to
invocate
That progeny of the grape
most profligate.
Come Dionysus! Consecrate
this holy place.

Alessandro:　I like that one; but what about the other god—the one you call the fair- haired one?

Maestro:　Ah yes, you're quite right. We should remember him, too.

Paolo:　No! Not more wine.

Maestro:　Then a little water will do. Dionysus will make ready and loosen our tongues for truth while Apollo provides for the clarity and order of what we say.

Sprinkling each young man on the head with water, the Maestro says:

Charioteer of the Sun
Draw your light across the sky
And lift our thoughts to heavenly realms.

Paolo:　Now we have been twice blessed by two different gods—whom do we obey?

Alessandro:　I would prefer to obey Dionysus. I'll sing the afternoon away and drink until my tongue turns purple.

Maestro:　As you often do, my boy, but it is time for you to sing a different song. Paolo has asked an interesting question, and like most interesting questions it will probably lead us through a labyrinth of thought.

Paolo: Can I withdraw the question?

Maestro: But why? It's a good question—a fundamental question which touches something very close to heart; it asks not only about what we "ought" to do, but how we are related to the gods.

Paolo: How can you be serious about gods that don't exist?

Maestro: But it was for no trivial reason, Paolo, that our cultural forefathers, the ancient Greeks, paid tribute to these two gods. Our gods are divine reflections of our own mortal faces—arrows of aspiration we shoot beyond ourselves; and our own faces—our image of ourselves—is a reflection of The Divine.

Paolo: When the Maestro has wine, he talks in circles.

Maestro: And we are taught, of course, to avoid the pitfalls of circular thought; but in order to understand what I have just said, we should distinguish between two kinds of circularity: the first kind we should indeed avoid and is used only to deviate from the truth and destroy good conversation; but the second circularity is a motion which characterizes the 'essence' of thought itself and, thereby, nourishes all real understanding.[3]

Alessandro: I'm not sure I understand either one. Also, I'm not sure about what you mean by the essence of something.

Maestro: The word 'essence' points to a difficult and much disputed concept with a long and tedious history—a history that now, alas, is no longer heard.

Paolo: You mean it's a dead concept, don't you?

3. Heidegger calls the second kind of circularity a Hermeneutic circle; it simply means that all thought emerges out of an interpretational horizon, or field, which is understood prior to our scientific or objective comportment to the world.

Maestro: Not quite dead—but lying forgotten in fallow ground, waiting to be revitalized—waiting for someone to breathe life back into it so it can once again respond.

Alessandro: Then let's revive it and see what it means.

Maestro: Let me try. When we look around us, we can see that ordinary objects become most useful when they are in their own environment—when they are not just used by us indiscriminately, but allowed to be where they belong. What, for instance, will happen if you put these pruning shears in the drying shed?

Alessandro: If we leave them there, they will soon rust and decompose.

Maestro: And fall into disuse?

Alessandro: Yes.

Maestro: Where then do they belong in order to become most fully what they are?

Alessandro: They belong in your hands, in order to be used in cutting back those trees.

Maestro: And that plough?

Alessandro: It belongs in the field digging up the ground, and this hat belongs on my head

Paolo: And this wine belongs in a barrel and is meant to be drunk! And... and you are meant to play the fool for Maestro's questions.

Alessandro: *e vero*, Maestro?

Maestro: Not at all! You took a risk and answered rightly, and in so doing acted wisely. You have a good and open heart,

Alessandro, and have understood the meaning of essence.

Alessandro: I have?

Maestro: Yes. As you have said, the 'essence' of a thing is not exactly identifiable with the actual thing itself, but also includes its possibilities—the total environment or 'circumstance' to which the thing belongs.[4]

Alessandro: That's exactly what I meant.

Maestro: Put another way, the essence of something includes the region in which both man and thing dwell.

Alessandro: Where it's at home?

Maestro: Yes, the place in which it flowers and becomes itself most fully and can, therefore, be most useful, and do its best work. But we were previously speaking about the essence of thinking. When, then, does thinking do its best work?

Alessandro: When we think hard.

Maestro: And what are we thinking about when we are thinking most diligently?

Alessandro: I suppose we're thinking about certain problems.

Maestro: And there are different kinds of problems, are there not?

Alessandro: Yes.

Maestro: Some that can be solved with the available tools we have— like puzzles with missing pieces: how to get from one place to another, or predict a causal relation from one thing to

---

4.   The Maestro is obviously familiar with Heidegger's *Being and Time* and Ortega's *Meditations on Quixote:* "I am myself plus my circumstances." Where Plato thought of the essence as the being of a thing—as its idea or form, Heidegger thinks of it as the historical context and prereflective understanding of the thing.

another; and then there are problems that cannot be resolved definitively and are of their very nature problematic.

Alessandro: Which can't be solved?

Maestro: Not in the same way, nor completely. There are problems and ideas which when solved help us get around and make life easier; ...and then there are beliefs and ideas upon which we will stake our lives! These are vital questions and therefore dangerous—ideas about what is "just", "good", or what is most "beautiful" and "true". About and around these ideas, philosophers can only circle like a hungry Gyrfalcon.[5]

Paolo: That is exactly why we should stick to what is practical and useful to us—stuff we can figure out! Your kind of thinking can only be about values and opinions, which are different for different people and can never be proved or answered.

Maestro: No, not finally answered. In fact, it is the temptation to closure, which poses the greatest danger. With vital questions, thinking must be vigilant and on the move around its target.

Alessandro: I know! That's what Socrates did. He would ask questions and give answers, and ask more questions, and go round and round until his opponents would get dizzy and tired of it—what were they called?

Paolo: Sophists!...and philosophers have been going in circles ever since. I don't see how this kind of thinking is useful at all. What possible good can come from something that gets nothing accomplished; and furthermore, what does it have to do with the gods?

---

5.   The allusion to the Royal Gyrfalcon is used by Ortega as a description of the mind of the philosopher, which circles in widening gyres around its object as prey. See: Jose Ortiga Y Gasset, *What is Philosophy* "Norton and Company, New York 1964" Chapter 7.

Maestro: Before I answer that, we should talk about the kind of circular thinking we should avoid—less we, in the course of our inquiry, fall victim to its snares. You, Paolo, should know this kind well.

Paolo: How's that?

Maestro: In the old country, before your parents sent you here to live with your uncle, you were studying for the bench—to be *un avvocato* as we say—a lawyer, is that right?

Paolo: Yes, before I got into some trouble at school.

Maestro: I am familiar with your problem, and it is unfortunate that we share the same fate; but tell me, when you studied law, were you not taught how to discredit the witness and question him in such a way as to confuse him and eventually lead him into contradiction?

Paolo: That was our job. It's the easiest thing in the world to learn—I mean, most anybody can be made to contradict himself.

Alessandro: Show us, Paolo?

Maestro: Yes, please do.

Paolo: All right, I would like to call Alessandro to the stand.

Alessandro: Swear me in!

Paolo: Never mind that! Answer my questions with a yes or no. Have you stopped your life of running around and constantly being in trouble?

Alessandro: Yes—I, er, I mean—

Maestro: I object! I will help you out Alessandro. That's very good, Paolo. You've already put Alessandro in a very bad light;

for no matter how he answers, he will incriminate himself. Give us another example of this method.

Paolo: There was some missing fruit from the store house last week—was there not?

Alessandro: Yes.

Paolo: Were you in the storehouse last week on Tuesday?

Alessandro: Yes.

Paolo: Now, the guilty person must be the person who was in the storehouse on Tuesday—right?

Alessandro: Yes.

Paolo: You, Alessandro, were in the store house on Tuesday.

Alessandro: Yes, but—

Paolo: So, it is obvious that you are the guilty person.

Alessandro: Wait! There's something wrong here.

Maestro: There certainly is, and at another time I will explain how Aristotle heroically and almost single-handedly refuted this kind of thinking; but for the moment it is enough to see that Paolo has cleverly presented circumstantial evidence, which as the word indicates, is an argument based not directly on the facts in question, but on what stands around them.

Alessandro: But how is this circular?

Maestro: It is circular because Paolo has tried to reach his conclusion from something he already put his mind to in the first premise namely, that you, Alessandro, are guilty.

Alessandro: So if I say "yes" to his first questions, I am convicted in the conclusion and would probably lose my job. There must be some trick here.

Paolo: The trick is that the person being questioned must only answer by a "yes" or "no".

Maestro: And as you know, most things in life are not one way or another, but must be qualified in some way.

Alessandro: That's right, there could have been a hundred people in and out of that storehouse last Tuesday—it wasn't me—really!

Maestro: We believe you, Alessandro. But we now see that there is a kind of thinking which intends to confuse and confound, taking what a person says and turning it back upon itself. The object of this kind of thought is not to be in search of truth, but to establish a point already decided upon.

Paolo: But the kind of legal thinking, which I have given examples of—this first kind of circularity you talk about—,is a very useful kind of thinking. I mean, it accomplishes what one sets out to do—like convicting Alessandro!

Maestro: Yes, it gets the job done if one develops the right techniques and methods—the effective 'means' to reach an already decided 'end'. We can call this strategic thinking. But is it thinking at its best,—is it true thinking?

Paolo: I would assume that thinking is thinking as long as it solves what it intends to do.

Maestro: Could there not, however, be types of thinking which are deficient in some way? Let me ask you something concerning what we talked about earlier—about the essence of thinking.

Paolo: Go ahead.

Maestro: When are you most pleased with your thinking?

Alessandro: Like Paolo says, I am most pleased when I have figured something out, or accomplish what I set out to do.

Paolo: And that's not too frequent, either.

Maestro: It may be, Paolo, that the few times we think well, far outweigh the many times we think deficiently. But regardless, you would say that thinking is most thoughtful when it solves something?

Alessandro: Yes.

Maestro: And this means when it uncovers something and comes to rest at the truth.

Alessandro: Yes, that's it!

Maestro: So, thinking belongs in some way to the truth,—but is at its best when it is in service to the truth and not when it just serves us; thinking should not just stop when it accomplishes what we want, but should be given its head and allowed to wander to and fro in search of the truth?

Paolo: But if we do that we will be in danger of letting our thoughts run wild and completely out of our control.

Maestro: There is always that risk, but herein lies the art of thinking. Have you ever gone horseback riding into the countryside and got so caught up in the rhythm of the gallop, and the sight of quickly passing landscapes that you quite suddenly find yourself lost?

Paolo: No—not really.

Alessandro: Yes, that did happen to me—it was just the other day that...

Paolo: That you got lost again. You are always getting lost because you are daydreaming and don't know where you are going.

Maestro: Much like thinking, it seems; for if you are not lost, if you already know where you are, there can be nothing to find out. But tell me, Alessandro, what did you do?

Alessandro: I just let go of the reins and the old stallion came right back to the orchard where he belongs.

Maestro: So, you guided your horse by feeling where he wanted to go, and gently let him have his way, in accordance with his nature.

Alessandro: Yes, that's what I did.

Maestro: It seems then, that the art of horseback riding, if it is to be an art, must respect and stay close to the nature and essence of the horse; and in this case, the nature of the horse is to somehow be aware of a larger field of reference and where the barn is. Now, what about the art of thinking? To what does it belong, and to what must it stay close?

Alessandro: It should stay close to—a...

Paolo: Thinking should stay in your head, Alessandro, where it belongs!

Maestro: That, *caro Paolo*, would be true for the chemicals and nerves in the brain, but not for thought; if thoughts and thinking were fixed within the parameters of your skull and reduced to being identical with the brains neural system, it would be much like confining the horse to the barn.

Alessandro: ...and like a bird in a cage...

Maestro: Yes Alessandro! And one can say that the brain through its complexification and creation of thought has found a way of opening itself to a much larger field of being.

Alessandro: Like a fish that becomes aware of the water?

Maestro: Exactly! Just as our own mind swims in the historical sea of ideas.

Paolo: Before we are carried away by runaway horses and birds and fish, we should remember what started this conversation.

Alessandro: I know; The Maestro said that we were reflections of the gods, and the gods were reflections of ourselves,—or something like that.

Maestro: Paolo then accused me of circular thinking. And I said there was a kind of circularity, which is not true to the essence of thought, and one that is.

Alessandro: And the kind of thinking Socrates did was circular in a good way because it went around in search of the truth—right?

Maestro: Yes, so if the first kind of thinking we discussed— 'strategic' thinking, which is a means to an already decided upon end—the second Socratic type can be called 'probative'.

Alessandro: I know! Because Socrates was poking around for the truth.

Maestro: For instance, Alessandro: if one wants to make a lot of money, then one needs some kind of plan or strategy, but whether this pursuit is a "good" thing as an end is another question.

Paolo: And that's the problem! We know now that the ideas that Socrates was examining—like "Justice," the "Good" and the "Beautiful"—are values and cannot be understood as facts! They boil down to just what people like or dislike; they are just opinions!

Maestro: Yes, but you would agree, Paolo, that we often desire things that are not "good" for us?

Paolo: Of course!

Maestro: And that's what Socrates would show. His thought went around in a dialectical fashion—a way of examining an opinion by showing the various problems and contradictions, which may arise. In some way an opinion, or belief, we hold to be true without examination is much like what the Greeks called a '*pharmakon*'.

Alessandro: A medicine?

Paolo: A poison!

Maestro: You are both right. A *pharmakon* was for the Greeks both a cure and a poison. The dialectical method was for Socrates a kind of therapy—one that cures the mind of fixed ideas, which can be dangerous. So Socrates would draw out the concept or opinion, its poisonous aspects—its internal contradictions—in hope of taking care of the soul.

Paolo: But you have yet to show how this round about method gets us anywhere—and why we should be allowed to break the "Law of Contradiction" and have it both ways about these kinds of ideas.

Maestro: We must be very careful when we invoke the "Law of Contradiction"—a venerable law without which the very foundations of our civilization would crumble and fall into chaos. But it is one thing to use this law in search of the truth, and quite another to abuse it.

Alessandro: What exactly is this law?

Paolo: That nothing can both "be" and "not be" at the same time and place.

Alessandro: That sounds right. We can't say that the wine is here and not here, or can we?

Maestro: We'll see. Paolo said earlier that it was easy to make a person contradict himself in this manner. Could you give us another of your fine examples?

Paolo: Gladly. Suppose Alessandro said that "all men desire justice," and then later admits, as he must, that there are individuals who are unjust. Are men just or are they unjust—which is it?

Alessandro: That's not fair!

Maestro: Have no fear Alessandro, for reason tells us that we should not try and apply what is meant to be a general truth about justice to every particular case. As I said before, there are certain questions which by their very nature are problematic and cannot be answered by a "this" or "that" or a "yes" or "no." Alessandro must be allowed to break free of this vicious circle and explain how it is that man can be both just and unjust; and if he does, he will gain a better understanding—one which does not go back and forth between two frozen opposites, but stays true to the dynamic nature of the question.

Paolo: Now you are suggesting that we disobey the "Law of Contradiction" and wander about in our thinking.

Maestro: Not at all. We should rather learn to apply this law where it does its best work.

Paolo: And where might that be?

Maestro: Why, it works wonders in the world of numbers and signs that must by their very nature stay fixed in their meaning. This clarity is important for dealing with 'matters of fact'.

Alessandro: And why is this?

Maestro: So they can be used to calculate, predict, and store information. If we are to wrestle from nature her innermost secrets—make her obey our commands,—then we cannot be whimsical with our concepts, having them change and shift their meaning from one moment to the next. When we use language in this exact manner, and numbers and signs are part of language, we are able to solve certain problems and preserve their solutions for posterity. This use of language is necessary for understanding nature and stabilizing civilization but is, nevertheless,—formal and abstract.[6]

Alessandro: What do you mean? Words are real.

Maestro: Yes, but in a different way from the vitality of life itself. Language is a way the flow of life is stopped and caught in order to be seen and thought about. The, word "tree" represents all of these leafy fruit bearing things in this orchard, but is not one of them—just as the number "two" is not the thing it represents.

Alessandro: How's that again?

Maestro: Take a look at these trees, they will blossom, bear fruit and eventually die—our concept of "tree" will not. In its vital reality, this tree is both living and dying, and growing new shoots as it drops its fruit to the ground; it is, one might say, a living contradiction.

Paolo: So you are saying that the "Law of Contradiction" does not apply to living things?

Maestro: Not exactly. It applies to them quite well when we want to understand life in a certain manner.

Paolo: In what manner?

---

6. Here, Maestro is trying to explain how modern science is born with the discoveries of Galileo and Descartes,—how that is, the formal world of geometry with its axioms and symbolic notation are understood and predict the movement of nature.

Maestro: When we want to categorize and control life—to securely hold it down for a moment in order to gain some rest from life's ceaseless ebb and flow—when we want to view life abstractly, as we must do from time to time in order to understand it.

Alessandro: I get it! We are holding down life with words and concepts... and numbers, and the "Law of Contradiction"— which says that "this" must be "this" and "that" must be "that;" but life is more like the mud in this irrigation ditch: when I try and grab it, it squeezes through my fingers.

Maestro: Bravo! Alessandro. What a profound irony we have now come upon.

Alessandro: What irony?

Maestro: The irony, Alessandro, is that in order to see life more clearly, we must sometimes detach ourselves from it and live somewhat abstractly. And it was precisely for this reason that the Greeks gave thanks to Apollo,—the god, or *theos*, who gives man the ability to see in light as a god would see, that is, theoretically. Like the discovery of the New World, the Greeks opened up and explored the theoretical space of reason where formal symbols with univocal meaning work in a most beautiful way.

Alessandro: But we can't catch all of life in this way can we? Isn't there always that part that slips through our fingers?

Maestro: Yes, the vital and therefore problematic part—and that is why the Hellenes invoked the name of the other god- Dionysus, the god of wine and revelry.

Paolo: Now we are back to the gods again.

Maestro: So we are. It seems we have let our ideas have their way and have wandered back to our place of departure; but this time we will view things from a higher vantage point—one like the widening gyre of our falcon.

Paolo: What do you mean?

Maestro: We have come full circle, but in the process have uncovered some new terrain, which will help us understand what I said before.

Alessandro: That the gods are reflections of ourselves, and also the other way around?

Maestro: Exactly! You see, the Greeks discovered something about the nature of man, which was quite paradoxical and wonderful.

Alessandro: Tell us what it was.

Maestro: For the first time, standing in the full light of the Mediterranean day, these children of the gods discovered the radiant and awesome power of reason. They knew the arrogant optimism of mortals allowed for a moment into heavenly realms,—but only for a moment—for at the same time they also smelled the wild bloom of life and felt the strange and mysterious attraction of the Earth, pulling them down into her forbidden darkness.[7]

Alessandro: And that's why they also worshiped Dionysus?

Maestro: Yes—the god who rules the vital procreative side of life, which still remains elusive to the eye of Reason and the "Law of Contradiction."

---

7. An extended note is needed here to explain the center of Heideggerian thought to which the Maestro refers: We usually translate the Greek word *aletheia* as truth in terms of the agreement (*adequatio*), or correspondence between statements/symbols and things—much like the way a map represents the earth. Heidegger, however, thinks that the etymology of the word—literally 'out of', or not the "river of oblivion"—tells us of another way the Greeks understood the truth and being of their world. This 'coming fourth' out of hiddenness (*phusis*) is an "unconcealedness" which for Heidegger is a more primary disclosure of being—one which understands the hidden as ontologically inexhaustible.

Paolo: But what good is this if there are no gods?

Maestro: The important thing, Paolo, is how man understands himself and the nature of things in general. What the Greeks discovered was not only a contradiction in themselves, but a cosmic contradiction, that is, that there exists an orderly element in nature and a disorderly element—Logos and Fire, Reason and Chaos—and this most elemental truth they sanctified by the Holy names of Apollo and Dionysus.

Alessandro: So, Apollo is the god who lights up the world so we can grab it and hold it with words and numbers and other such things—while Dionysus is wild and hides in the mud where he can't be captured—is that it?

Maestro: Oh, Alessandro, that is certainly it! But Dionysus does have a weakness, which will enable us to lure him from his hidden earthly lair.

Alessandro: Good! Tell us this weakness, so when he does appear we can throw a net over him and hold him captive.

Maestro: His weak spot—for concerning man, even gods have weak spots—his vulnerability lies in his love of music, especially certain secret scales and rhythms which will drive him from the bushes into the open.

Alessandro: Then we will...

Maestro: Not capture him but circle around him with dance and song and a thinking that is more musical than logical—a thinking which stays closer to the vitality of life itself.

Paolo: I have so far been amused, but this has gone too far! I can certainly see how the gods are projections of how we fancy ourselves to be, but it makes no sense to say that we are reflections of the gods, since you cannot show that there are such gods; and furthermore , what you call the Dionysian or the unknown part of life can be found out sooner or later by logic or reason. Here I think I am in good company.

Alessandro: What company?

Maestro: Paolo, my young Apollonian friend, refers to none other than Descartes, Galileo, and all of so called modern science; they all agree on the rational nature of the world and the ability of reason to comprehend it. For the first time the cosmos would finally reveal its secrets and become fully transparent.

Paolo: And that I think is good enough! You have seen what obeying the "Law of Contradiction" and using the tools of reason can bring to man, but what is it that your kind of thinking—dialectical or probative thinking—brings? What can thinking, which goes back and forth indefinitely, ever give us?

Maestro: I see, Paolo, that you have learned much from your training and are a clear headed young man of the times; but what I have in mind is a different kind of thinking—one that questions the essence of thought itself and the possible consequences of its complete reduction to formal reason and calculation.

> *The Maestro rises from the orchard floor and looks to he sky.*

For now, we still have much work to do and many trees to prune   before   the   sun   goes   down.

Part Two

It is dark, and a dim, flickering light can be seen through the window of the old cottage by the creek. Paolo and Alessandro approach the door.

Alessandro: Maestro! It is me, Alessandro—and Paolo is here, too.

Maestro: My friends, what brings you here at this late hour?

Paolo: It is warm in our tent and Alessandro can't seem to calm down.

Alessandro: Neither can Paolo,—he keeps talking about his girl friend back home and...

Maestro: I understand. Nights such as this, when the air is heavy with moisture and the smell of ripening apricots,—such nights do indeed have strange effects upon our senses. I, too, was disturbed just now by memories of my home; but come in, and we will talk awhile.

Paolo: Yes, I would still like to know how we are reflections of the gods. As I said last time, I understand that the gods are projections of our highest ideals, and that these ideals are dependent upon how we understand ourselves and the world, but not how our self-understanding is dependent on the gods. I mean, you have yet to show how we are reflections of the gods.

Alessandro: Neither do I understand that, nor the part about the other kind of circular thinking.

Maestro: Then let me try and explain what I meant. When we think about anything, whether about the gods or something else, we are always involved in circular thinking.

Paolo: How's that?

Maestro: When we have a question about something—and all thinking is initiated by something questionable or problematic—our question presupposes that we know in someway, however dim, what it is that we are asking about.

Alessandro: That's right! How can I ask about something unless I know what I'm asking about? But if I know what I'm asking about,... why am I even asking? I'm confused.

Paolo: This is Plato's paradox of learning. But it is not necessary to say, as Plato did, that we could know what to ask about because our souls recollected this information from a previous existence.

Maestro: No, this is not necessary, but...

Paolo: We could better say that when we ask about something, we know about it in the way of making an educated guess, that is, we form a hypothesis—then we set out to prove it true or false.

Maestro: Nevertheless, the Divine Plato has put his finger on something quite interesting about the nature of thought. When we ask a question or form a hypothesis about what we don't know, we must always assume something that is not questioned.

Paolo: This you must explain.

Maestro: We can start with the question we have been talking about. For example, when you said the gods don't exist, you have already presumed the meaning of the word god and what it means for something to exist. How we understand notions such as these is rarely due to our own efforts at thinking, but is rather given to us by our circumstances.

Alessandro: What do these trees and things around us have to do with how we understand things?

Maestro: I don't mean by circumstance just one's physical surroundings, but the lived world in which we dwell— the context of life, which we all share. The very ordinary words we utter and the beliefs by which we live and die carry with them a silent but ever-present historical dimension. We find ourselves 'thrown' in the world, taking for granted a great many things we have inherited and have never questioned. So when we use certain words or pose certain questions, we always do so with the help of something previously understood. You might say, we must of necessity impose our previous understanding on what is to be understood.

Paolo: But this is exactly the kind of prejudice which science overcomes. When we think scientifically, we purposely withhold our personal beliefs and look only at the facts; and when we talk about these facts, we can change our language into mathematical symbols so that anyone in any place can understand them and perform the same experiments with the same results. This is why thinking must remain objective and overcome the kind of circularity you are talking about; and this is also why we should obey the "Law of Contradiction." I mean, we could not get very far if we said that πr^2 'is' the area of a circle and also 'is not' the area of a circle, or that the hydrogen atom both does and does not have an atomic weight of one.

Alessandro: Maestro, here I think I agree with Paolo. We could never know anything without this kind of scientific thinking.

Maestro: As I said previously, this is essential for knowing about the world in a certain way, or when dealing with "matters of fact."

Paolo: An unbiased and non-circular way!

Maestro: Here I'm afraid you're wrong. There seem to be two types of objective knowledge, but neither are free of bias or circularity.

Alessandro: Which two?

Maestro: Well, there is the method of Empirical Science with its principle of verifiability, and the Formal Sciences of mathematics and logic. But even with the exact nature of mathematics, we can show a kind of circularity at work. For example, when we say that 2+2 is equal to 4, we have merely said the same thing twice; that is, the concept of 4 is another way of saying 2+2; or when we say that πr^2 is the area of a circle, what we mean by circle is exactly πr^2. It does not make sense to contradict something that is true by definition; to say, in essence, that a triangle does not have three sides, when three sides are what a triangle must have if it is to be a triangle. These kinds of exact definitions account for the beautiful symmetry and functional elegance of the world of numbers and symbols, where corollaries and inferences flow necessarily from the fountainhead of axiomatic truths.[8]

---

8.   The Maestro is referring to the debate between Hume and Kant on the distinction between what Hume called **Relations of Ideas** (analytic statements) and **Matters of Fact** (synthetic statements): with the former, as in "bachelors are unmarried" the predicate term, 'unmarried', cannot be falsified without contradicting the subject term; but if one says "bachelors have blond hair," obviously the predicate can be verified or falsified. Hume held that Relations of Ideas (analytic statements) were tautological, or circular. What Whitehead called **Matters of Importance** (evaluative statements) are best handled by a dialectical method.

Alessandro: I'm not sure what you mean by axiomatic.

Maestro: An axiom is a first principle, which must be accepted before other truths can be deduced from it. If you accept as the definition of a circle that "all radii are equidistant from the center point," then the area can be calculated as πr^2; but, as you can see, this and many other geometrical truths which follow are dependent on one's first definition. What I mean is that the implications we draw are contained in the definitions we propose.

Alessandro: Now I am confused!

Paolo: I must admit that I am, too. What should we conclude from this?

Maestro: Only that it is the nature of thought to be in a circular relation to that which it thinks about; so in order to find out something about circles and squares, we must first know what these things are. In a quite peculiar way it is the essence of the square that sets its own limitations—tells us what and how much more we can know.

Paolo: Even if we accept this as true for mathematics, how can you say that science is circular—that it has presuppositions—if it starts by looking at the facts first?

Maestro: Science does get rid of certain kinds of presuppositions—prejudices and unwarranted beliefs that should be gotten rid of—but it cannot rid itself of certain other more fundamental presuppositions without destroying that which it sets out to do. The scientist can tell us that the real cause of malaria is not swamp gas, but he cannot question the nature of causality itself. It is quite strange that in order to know that one fact "causes" another, we must assume a principle which is itself not a fact—namely the "category" of causality, which Kant tells us is one of the conditions of possibility for understanding the world; and as such, it is 'a priori' or prior to understanding. You see these questions are for a different kind of science—a science that looks at the fundamental assumptions of thinking itself.

Alessandro: You mean Philosophy?

Maestro: Yes. When we look a bit deeper into the notion of causality, we may find that something which causes something else may also be effected in some way; so that causality may contain its own contrary; or we may even wonder if causality exists only in the mind of man, and not in nature at all.

Paolo: Well, I think one science is sufficient. The category of causality is merely a tool; and like all tools it is there to be used. If we stopped to ask whether a hammer was really there or how it was possible that it hit the nail; we would certainly never build a house. These kinds of questions get us nowhere and accomplish nothing.

Maestro: You are quite right. We will accomplish nothing in the way of making wheels turn or changing one substance into another; and yet, I find something quite miraculous in what you call these tools of understanding. Tell me, when you use a tool, like a hammer, do you know beforehand what it can do?

Paolo: Yes.

Maestro: And does not the hammer in some way dictate how much and in what manner something gets done?

Paolo: I don't know what you mean.

Maestro: I mean, if you are using a hammer, your house could only be made of nails and wood.

Paolo: I really don't see how...

Maestro: And when your house is finished, anyone could see it was built with a hammer?

Paolo: Yes, of course!

Maestro: The hammer, then, leaves its mark and sets the limitations on how the house is to be built. Now, you said that science uses such conceptual tools in its experiments and thinking, did you not?

Paolo: Yes.

Maestro: Well then, you must see that these so called objective experiments carry with them an army of ghostly presuppositions that set certain limitations on what and how something is to be known.

Paolo: No, I don't quite see...

Maestro: As we mentioned before, science must assume that the objects it looks at be not only causally related but must behave in a lawful and non-contradictory manner; and further, it is assumed that these objects are material in nature and exist independent of man in space and time. These notions and many others make up a total unquestioned picture of reality, which silently, but forcefully, allows by the kinds of questions it asks only certain answers.

Alessandro: Wait Maestro! I think I understand. You mean that the questions we ask are loaded like... like the dice we play with? I mean...

Paolo: I knew it!

Alessandro: I mean, that we can only find what we're already looking for.

Maestro: Amazing Alessandro! You will forgive this pun, but you have hit the nail on the head. The tools of science are used for measuring and establishing the laws of nature, and therefore, they will only find what is measurable and lawful in nature. So even here, with the strictest of information gathering, we find ourselves caught within the parameters of a certain kind of thinking—a thinking which is quite objective about everything but, its own method and its possible consequences.

Paolo: But why question a method, which works? All the concepts, categories, and ideas that you say are assumed, or 'a priori', are commonsensical and produce the best results.   .

Maestro: Yes, many fine results; and if our friends the scientists would stop to question such ideas, they would certainly not produce very much; yet, I cannot rest content with a kind of thinking which can only operate by assuming the platform on which it stands.

Paolo: Much like the way you stand on one limb in order to cut the one above you down?

Maestro: Yes, in very much the same way.

Paolo: Well Alessandro, it seems that the Maestro would not mind if we cut down the limb he stands on when he prunes his trees.

The young men laugh.

You see, Maestro, you are not being very practical when you question things which are quite commonsensical; it can only bring you some comical, or even disastrous end.

*The Maestro looks away and
thinks a moment about the
circumstances, which brought*

him to this orchard so far from home.

Maestro: What you say is true, and like all truths it strikes at the heart; still, there is something troublesome about man. Have you never heard the voice of the impractical self calling you away from your everyday business and daily chores—bidding you to strap wings to your back like Icarus and fly towards the sun?

Alessandro: Not really.

Paolo: And we know what happened to Icarus.

Maestro: Tell me Paolo, about this lady you were thinking about tonight—do you love her?

Alessandro grins and Paolo blushes.

Ah! Your heart has betrayed what your mind hides. It's quite impractical that you think of her when separated by thousands of miles. And if while she waits for you she fell into the wrong hands, would you...

Paolo: I would leave this place for home!

Maestro: Even though you know what danger awaits you there?

Paolo: Yes!

Maestro: How strange this is, Paolo, that man is freed by love from the tyranny of natural needs and carried beyond the bounds of common sense and security to risk, if necessary, his own life for the sake of what he believes to be "just" or "true".

Paolo: But what is strange in this? All creatures have a need to protect those things which they desire; what you call love is merely a matter of what we are inclined towards.

Maestro: We are certainly creatures with inclinations and needs, and as such are guided by the same invisible hand of necessity which directs all living things towards their survival, procreation, and finally towards their death. We share many such things with other creatures—creatures as beautiful as those wild game which come here at dusk to water; but there is much in man which is wilder still. When we are impassioned about learning or burn to know the "truth", just for the sake of knowing, we are no longer in "need," but in "love."

Paolo: I don't understand why it is necessary to draw a distinction between "love" and "need". For me, it is only a difference in degree. When you say, for instance, that man loves justice or truth, I would say that he needs these things for practical reasons—for his own survival.

Maestro: Do you mean to say that it is practical for man to need impractical things?

Paolo: I didn't say that.

Maestro: I wish you would have, for is it not the case, as you said, that "justice" and "truth" and other such concepts differ from man to man and from century to century—that they are not like facts found in nature which all men can readily agree upon, but are beliefs of a human kind?

Paolo: Yes,... values.

Maestro: Then surely it is quite peculiar that man can turn against the most practical of all needs—his own survival—and can, and does in fact, give up his very life for a belief—a mere idea about something. No, Paolo, we are not like these wild game who are caught in a web of cosmic practicality, prisoners of their drives and needs, we are a different kind of animal—a curious kind of animal who is free to turn against his own animality and thereby transfigure his basic needs into ideas and art. Yes, it is quite peculiar indeed that man can from time to time escape his needs— escape the animal chains, which bind him and become, if even for a short while, as playful and impractical as the gods.

Alessandro: I remember that Plato said we could either let the horses of our appetites and passions drive us downward or let love lift our souls to higher places...

Maestro: Yes, that we could transcend ourselves in some way through the power of eros. As I said a few days ago, we are the theoretical animal who, because he dares to break the law of gravity and fly higher and see more than any bird, must inevitably fall harder and lower than any beast. So although we can catch a glimpse of what a god might see, before our sight fades and our wings sputter and fail, we cannot for long sustain the godly view.[9]

Paolo: Quite comical!

Alessandro: Maestro, this is not comical but tragic—I mean, to come so close and then fail.

Maestro: I'm afraid you are both partially right; but remember, it is one thing to fly too high and lose ourselves amongst the clouds or burn up in the heat of the sun, and quite another thing to have the wings of a game hen, content to cluck and never fly at all.

Alessandro: Do you mean that the difference between comedy and tragedy is like the difference between a chicken and an eagle?

9.   That in Greek mythology Eros the god of love is married to Psyche, tells us that the psyche is understood as a desiring thing; and the 'object' of desire is what qualifies the type of character and the dynamics of the psyche—whether, that is, the soul is depleted by appetitive consuming, or finds its refuge in the eternal ideas.

Maestro: Not exactly! I only want to say that even though the comic gesture hides a tragic dimension—and the seriousness of tragedy often appears comical—it is still one thing to choose what is more than man in us, and quite another to be content with what is less.

Paolo: That's not much of a choice.

Maestro: But choose we must.

Paolo: And what if I choose to believe in nothing—to just take things as they are?

Maestro: Still a choice my boy, but one, which is doomed to be comical.

Paolo: Why is that?

Maestro: When you choose not to know and not to care, you will nevertheless be buffeted about like a dust particle in the wind, manipulated either by the concerns and beliefs of others or by your own prejudices and compulsions—like a puppet on the strings of fate dangling here below for the amusement of the gods.

Alessandro: Personally, I would cut the strings and be free of them.

Maestro: Then Alessandro, you, like Prometheus might pay the price for defying the gods. Because he loved man and brought the gift of fire, the gods nailed him to a precipice for an eternity of time.

Alessandro: I knew it! We are in all this mess because of love.

Maestro: We mortals are surely problematic, but it is rather because we are not ourselves in some way that we are capable of love and desire.

Alessandro: Out of our heads!

Paolo: Speak for yourself, Alessandro.

Maestro: No Paolo, I'm afraid Alessandro speaks for all of us. It would be better, however, to say that man can take a position for or against himself, and, therefore, must be in some way outside and beyond himself.

Alessandro: This I don't understand. I am just myself —a man.

Maestro: Yes, but the question is how you exist as a man. Are you a man the same way an animal is an animal?

Alessandro: In some ways.

Maestro: Precisely in what way?

Alessandro: Well, as far as we are animals, a certain part of our nature goes on without the least consent on our part, acting and doing things automatically—just as animals do.

Maestro: Perfectly in tune with the rest of the cosmos?

Alessandro: Yes...

Maestro: And when we do these things, do we have knowledge about what we do or is there a part of us which knows in a way which does not know?

Alessandro: Yes, that's it! Our animal nature knows how to do things by instinct, but does not know why it does so.

Maestro: So you would say that although animals know how to do much, they know nothing about what they do.

Alessandro: And they don't care to know either!

Maestro: Why do you think that's the case?

Alessandro: I don't know. They just are what they are.

Maestro: But man wants to know, does he not? He 'cares'.

Alessandro: Yes, man is always concerned with this or that.

Maestro: How very strange.

Alessandro: Why?

Maestro: Because man must not be what he is. If he were totally identical with himself, with what he is, he would be content not to know or care.

Alessandro: This does sound strange! But in what way is man not himself?

Maestro: When I said earlier that man is somehow outside of himself, I meant that he is always looking at himself problematically and at a distance. Every moment that we are, we are not only a reflection of that moment, but are also off toward the future.[10]

Paolo: For once I am with Alessandro. Neither do I understand how that is possible.

Maestro: It is possible, Paolo, because we are temporal beings. Were you not aware at the moment you were asking that question that you were asking it? And do you not wait in anticipation of an answer and wonder about what you will say?

Paolo: Yes, of course.

---

10. Kant laid the groundwork for Heidegger when he said that time and space were the conditions of possibility for experience of the sensory world. For Heidegger time is not a category or schema of organization but constitutes our very being. Dasein (being there) is Heidegger's word for the being that is ek-static and thrown open to the future.

Maestro: So in some sense man is always worried and concerned about not only what he "is" but also what he "will be" in the future; and because he is aware of himself in this way, a self reflecting upon itself, man is doomed to be a question to himself—an incomplete self in search of himself.

Alessandro: And animals, since they are complete and satisfied with themselves, do not reflect upon themselves and ask what it is that they are doing. They have no questions and do not want to know.

Maestro: Yes, and because they are what they are, and feel no need for anything beyond themselves, they seek no truth, nor long to know. It's odd, but in this regard our friends the animals are much closer to the gods than we are.

Paolo: How so? I can see how man is like a god in some ways and like an animal in other ways, but how is it possible for an animal to be like a god?

Maestro: We must be careful not to talk in a blasphemous way concerning things which are Holy, but if the gods are to be gods, they must be infinite and eternal, and, therefore, capable of seeing and knowing all things. It would make no sense to say a god was incomplete and lacked something or worried about something as we mortals do.

Alessandro: No, that would not be right.

Maestro: So the gods do not need anything beyond themselves; they are complete and self-sufficient and need only amuse themselves with what they already know will happen.

Paolo: A divine theater where the gods watch the folly of those trying to know more than they can.

Maestro: That would be folly. But what about our animal friends who are locked blindly within nature's laws, what do they need beyond their natural needs?

Alessandro: Nothing.

Maestro: It seems, then, that the gods are complete and all-knowing, and animals are complete and un-knowing. The wild game we see around us live in unity with themselves. They are un-reflective and non-questioning, neither a problem to themselves nor others. This is their blessing; for unlike men, they cannot lie to themselves, to others, nor to the gods.

Alessandro: And since the gods can do whatever they please, neither can they sin—right?

Maestro: Precisely! They are totally without boundaries and, therefore, free from all penalty of transgression. Only in heaven or here on the beastial floor can beings maintain a primal innocence—an innocence beyond good or evil.

Paolo: And what of man?

Maestro: He is an appearance of what the Greeks knew quite well when they invoked the; names of Apollo and Dionysus...

Alessandro: That we can know like the gods, but not everything; but we are still stuck on earth like the animals.

Maestro: And it is because we are caught somewhere between god and beast, unsure of our own nature, that we tirelessly seek to know—leaving no stone unturned as we search through all things both near and far for some clue to ourselves and our destiny. This is why we cannot, and must not, leave unquestioned even the most practical and commonsensical everyday things, but must saw away the very limbs on which we stand.

Paolo: I see we are back to the gods and sawing limbs out from under ourselves. I understand the need to question, but I maintain that certain kinds of questions—philosophical questions that only go round in circles—lead us nowhere; it would be far wiser to forget them and concentrate on some useful problems.

Maestro: I suppose we should. But I have in mind here a different kind of usefulness—one which is more proper to man; but we have talked late into the night and tomorrow we have much work to do. Before I say goodnight to you, I can reply that in matters of the heart and mind it is far better for man to fall into the circular vortex of truth than to stand secure in error and self-satisfaction.

Paolo: That you will surely have to explain.

Part Three

The sun is setting on the orchard and the Maestro is watching irrigation water flow through the rutted ditches surrounding the trees.

Alessandro: Maestro, Paolo is roasting the rabbit we caught today and wants you to eat with us; he says you did not explain yourself very well last night.

Maestro: Then by all means I shall try again, and bring with me a different kind of food.

Alessandro: Good! Have you made dessert?

Maestro: No, but something just as sweet to me—nourishment for the mind.

Alessandro: Oh that. We could have used something more like gelato or torta... I'm so tired of fruit.

The old man and the boy walk through the orchard to a campsite situated in a clearing with a small fire burning within a circle of stones.

Paolo: You are just in time Maestro—the sacrifice is about to begin.

Paolo jumps to his feet with a skewered roasted rabbit in his hand and thrusts it upward to the sky.

Paolo: Maestro, who is the god who rules over our stomachs?

Maestro:	I'm not sure of that one.

Paolo: Oh, well—to an unknown god then:
Let the smoke from this fire burn
and lift the scent of
this delicious rabbit to the
nostrils of the god who will
bless our appetites.

Maestro: Bravo! But I hope your meter does not offend the gods and leave us with indigestion.

*They all laugh and sit down to their
meal of meat and wine.*

Paolo: The season will soon be over and Alessandro and I will be leaving for school; but before we go you must clear up some puzzling things you said.

Maestro: I will do my best; but what is it that bothers you?

Paolo: To start with, I can agree that the gods are certainly our creations, but you have implied that we are somehow their creations—reflections of the gods, as you say; this you have not really explained; nor have you showed what usefulness is derived from such circular thinking.

Alessandro: Philosophical thinking?

Paolo: Yes, more specifically what the Maestro calls dialectical thinking which can never stand on firm ground but continually turns around like a dog at its tail.

Alessandro: And asks questions which have no answers; and then there's the part about love... and...

Maestro: Please! I think I have enough to start with. These notions you mention are all connected but I see we will have to go around again and try this time to catch our prey.

He pauses a moment.

When we talked of the ancient gods, Apollo and Dionysus, we saw how they represented an essential predicament of man—the situation of being caught between god and animal, enduring the tensions between reason and instinct theory and life; and further, that the two regions which these gods rule over require their own particular kind of thinking.[11]

Alessandro: Would you go over that again?

Maestro: Yes. You remember we said that there was a kind of thinking which strives for lucidity and exactness and must obey the "Law of Contradiction" if it is to capture and hold the flow of life.

Alessandro: Now I remember! Scientific thinking, which belongs to Apollo and uses signs and numbers.

Maestro: Yes, signs and symbols that can only keep their meanings exact by being empty and abstract—formal signs, which stand above the content of life and time ready to be filled by anyone in any place.

Alessandro: Like algebraic equations?

Paolo: Which, as we must admit, accomplish a great many things.

Maestro: Many things indeed! But there is also a way of thinking that we cannot help but indulge in—a thinking that

---

11. Plato taught that the being of the human being was "*metaxic:*" that is, that the psyche, or soul, experiences the tension of being 'in between' the beginning and the beyond, the arche and the eschaton, the temporal and eternal—between animals and God. For a wonderful exposition of this see: Eric Voegelin, "Plato and Aristotle" in vol. III of *Order and History*.

concerns the vital concrete context in the midst of which man finds himself.

Alessandro: So there is a kind of thinking that starts outside of life and one that is inside.

Maestro: Yes, in a way. But it would be more accurate to say that one kind of thinking—the objective kind—is done from the **third person** point of view, which allows verification and falsification, by others; the other kind consists of descriptions made from the **first person** concerning human existence.[12]

Alessandro: And that in real life we can't be satisfied with equations but have to 'decide' what is right or wrong, or what we should or should not believe. Is this what this kind of thinking is about?

Maestro: Yes, and if you remember, we made a distinction between **Formal Thinking** which deals with logical and mathematical relations, and **Empirical Thinking** which deals with 'matters of fact'?

Alessandro: Yes.

Maestro: Now we must add a third kind of thinking which concerns itself with **Matters of Importance** and how we evaluate them—what we called dialectical thinking.

Paolo: And this is the central problem I mean, the question as to the usefulness of this way of thought. After all, what I value—what is important for me—may not be what is important for anybody else.

Maestro: Yes, I know, but if you will bear with me a while longer, I will try to make this clear. Did we not say that when a

12. Here the Maestro is referring to **phenomenology**—the movement represented by Husserl and Heidegger—which seeks to describe the direct and invariant structures of mind and existence.

thing is most essentially itself it is most useful?

Alessandro: Yes.

Maestro: And when is a thing most essentially itself?

Alessandro: When it does what it is supposed to do.

Maestro: And as we said, in order for a thing to do what it is supposed to do, it must be where it belongs, that is, it must be in the environment that is proper to it—its domain.

Alessandro: Yes, we said that the pruning shears belong in your hands in order to cut the branches, and the plough should be in the field doing its work.

Maestro: Where it is most useful?

Alessandro: Yes.

Maestro: Then tell me, what is most essential to being human? What most dearly belongs to us and to what do we in turn belong?

Alessandro: I'm not sure I know what you mean.

Maestro: What is it, Alessandro, that we have which makes us human—that which belongs to us alone and not to gods or beasts.

Paolo: Man is the "rational animal."

Maestro: Actually, Paolo, Aristotle said that man is the *zoon politikon*—the animal, who in order to fulfill its essence, must be in conversation with others about the important issues of the polis which constitutes the larger psyche. This more primary concern must be addressed through the give and take of practical reasoning in order to secure a place for being rational. But, regardless, what do you mean by rational?

Paolo: That he can weigh things out before he acts, that is, that he calculates and reasons.

Maestro: And in order to think, man must break the binds of instinct and reflect upon what he is doing?

Paolo: Yes.

Maestro: Well, since gods already know everything and beasts know but don't reflect, you might say that man is the only creature with a problem—or better, a creature whose very being is problematic! And wouldn't you say that this condition is prior to any project one undertakes?

Paolo: I suppose you could put it that way.

Maestro: And why not! It is precisely because the human kind of being is essentially a being-in-question, incomplete and always on the way, that he can be and think. And this, *mio regazzi*, is our crown of thorns—that is, that we are a kind of animal who wonders about our own animality and in so doing transcends the animal kingdom and becomes the philosophical animal.

Alessandro: What about the thorny part?

Paolo: That's the part where we make up all kinds of plans and schemes in order to get out of this situation...and then kill each other. Wouldn't it be better to call our selves the dangerous animal with tools, weapons, and opinions!

Maestro: Ah! I see Paolo that you have read the Antigone where Sophocles refers to man as "*to dienotaton*"—the strange and dangerous creature who wanders over land and sea in an endless quest.

Alessandro: How about the lost animal?

Maestro: Precisely so!

Alessandro: Will we ever find ourselves?

Maestro: We will find ourselves only when we confront our essential nature.

Alessandro: And you say that our essential nature is to be lost—to wander about and be a problem?

Maestro: Exactly!

Alessandro: Then we can only find ourselves when we find out that we are lost?

Paolo: Now the Maestro has succeeded in turning everything on its head: Alessandro is now the perfect man because he is almost always lost, and science has become most useless because it finds things out.

Maestro: On the contrary. I said that establishing facts and answering questions is very useful, but is only possible because man is first of all a question to himself.

Paolo: Let me get this straight. You said the essence of man has something to do with what best characterizes his nature, or, as you put it, with what belongs to him... which is to be lost?

Maestro: Yes. To be a problem.

Paolo: So how, pray tell, is it useful for man to be lost?

Maestro: If these birds did not build their nests, and the gods did not take care of their divine duties; they would be quite useless, would they not?

Paolo: Yes, of course.

Maestro: So, too, must man be heedful of that which claims his being, that is, he must be careful to go about the business, which is proper to him.

Paolo: The business of being lost?

Maestro: Which also means the business of being found. You see if what belongs to man as being closest to him is his own problematic being, then man most closely belongs to that which is most problematic itself—to the 'why' and 'how' of all that there is. We are, Paolo, claimed by Being itself. It is there, lost in the heart of what is most wonderful and inexhaustible, that man finds his proper abode.

Paolo: And this you say is useful? That's quite strange.

Maestro: Not if we give it some thought. We said that the essence of something cannot be exclusively identified with the thing itself, but must include the world around, or the circumstance of the thing, which enables it to fulfill itself. Is this not right?

Alessandro: Yes, just like a fish.

Paolo: What's that?

Alessandro: A fish! A fish, in order to be a fish, has to have water—

Maestro: And what about humans?

Alessandro: We have food and air and...

Maestro: Yes, yes. These are necessary conditions for us as they are for all living creatures; but they are not sufficient! Once again, how do we differ from animals?

Alessandro: You said, we have a problem that makes us think a lot.

Maestro: And what, Alessandro, does it take to think?

Alessandro: A brain and some ideas, I suppose.

Maestro: You suppose right; for just as a bird moves through the air and a fish is most itself in the water, man dwells most suitably in the world of ideas—a world without which man could not see or know that he knows, or know that he does not know, but would sink back to the level of instinct.

Alessandro: So if man does not think he cannot be himself, and would be useless.

Maestro: Useless, in the most profound sense of becoming enslaved to the ideas of others.

Paolo: I agree that thinking belongs to man, but...

Maestro: But you hesitate to say that man belongs to the world of ideas.

Paolo: Yes, I don't think it is necessary to put it that way.

Maestro: I see. Then do you think, *caro mio*, that we spontaneously come up with ideas and apply them will-nilly, when and where we want... that we land on earth with an empty head or "tabula rasa" as John Locke said, and start from scratch over and over again? Or can we not help being thrown into a world of ideas, like it or not, sink or swim—thrown into a world which is already there and loaded with ideas expressed as 'Matters of Importance'?

Paolo: Yes,... but...

Maestro: Then in some way thinking, and the ideas which have been thought about, lay claim to our being as the place in which we must move about; and this movement of ideas, and the traces they leave, is what we mean by the cultural-historical life of humanity—the life to which we are born and inherit as our own. So, isn't it a 'Matter of Importance' that we stay close to that to which we belong?

Alessandro.   Very important! And if we don't move about in the world of ideas very well, we would be like a fish out of water or a bird in a cage.

Maestro: Unfortunately so. We would be useful to someone else— but not to ourselves.

Paolo: All right then. Thinking belongs to man and man belongs to the historical world of ideas—the world of thought; but this does not convince me that thinking should be concerned with what you call the "problematic" itself, or the mysterious, or with ideas which always remain questionable.

Maestro: No, I didn't think it would. Let me then return once again to the question about the essence of thinking. To what did we say thinking belonged if it is to be thinking in its fullest sense?

Alessandro: To the "Truth". Not to that kind of thinking which convicted me of something I didn't do.

Maestro: And the "Truth", by its very nature must surely be what is most worthy of our thoughts—what is most thought provoking—is it not?   .

Alessandro: Yes, it seems so. But what is it about the "Truth" which makes it so interesting—so thought provoking, as you say?

Maestro: When we say that someone has spoken some truth, we usually mean he has 'revealed' what 'is' the case—would you agree?

Alessandro: Yes.

Maestro: Then it follows that the total "Truth" must be the total revelation of what 'is'—of Being—of all that there is.

Alessandro: I suppose so.

Maestro: But since we mortals are finite and limited to an understanding which cannot see beyond our own perspective and time, Being can only offer itself to man in different aspects—in ways in which man is ready to receive it.

Alessandro: You mean that we can never get the total "Truth" because we can't see all that there is.

Maestro: No, not unless we could continuously see as the gods who are eternal and outside of time and change. So it is of the nature of Truth to be inexhaustible and to reveal only so much of what is—only so much of Being.

Alessandro: Then all the rest of Being must be hidden.

Maestro: Yes, and since we cannot see all things with an eternal eye, our thinking must always be provoked about what conceals itself and lies hidden from view. It is to the unknown that we are drawn like a moth to the flame— drawn to that which is not only the most fundamental ground of our being, but the Being of all things. That is why certain kinds of questions—vital questions which concern those things which are most problematic and near to the heart of man—can never be resolved once and for all, but must instead stay close to, and be guided by, the essence of Truth.

Paolo: Which is?

Maestro: ...to always present itself as a partial disclosure of what is and not a final answer—always a further question. In this way the "Truth" will be most truthful when it is allowed to point to what is necessarily concealed and hidden from view and not when it is forced to be something final and complete. Our thinking, then, will be guided by the ''Truth" when it pays proper respect to the nature of Being by never supposing that Being can be totally captured or subdued. The 'Truth" must always be allowed to reveal more and more of Being by posing itself as a further question. In this way Truth is allowed to be what it is as the endless dialectic of revealment and concealment.

Alessandro: And we can do this by going around and around the same questions in the circular way you were talking about before?

Maestro: Yes.

Alessandro: A way of thinking which has no answer?

Maestro: No, not quite. There will be many answers given as we spiral around our problem—answers that will turn into further questions and push us upward to the next higher circle where there will be more answers and still further questions.

Alessandro: But it will be the same problem, won't it?

Maestro: Yes, except that each mind like each generation, will occupy a different rung of the spiral, and will, therefore, have a different view of the same eternal problems.

Alessandro: You mean problems like 'Truth", "Beauty", and "Goodness"?

Maestro: Yes, vital problems which should always concern us.

Alessandro: Then what we want is the best possible view of these matters—the best rung of the spiral.

Maestro: Bravo Alessandro! And to attain this we should think in a way which aspires to the circle that included the ones below it and, therefore, offers us the most comprehensive view of the problem.

Alessandro: And if we don't, we will be, as I said before, like a fish out of water, or a bird in a cage.

Maestro: Just like a bird, Alessandro,—a bird enslaved and unable to fly. What is useful to us, Paolo, a usefulness beyond the mere use of things which is of course necessary, is that we become free for what must essentially belongs to us—that we become free for the Truth.[13]

Paolo: Humans belong to the Truth you say? How ironic then that most of us are liars and spend most of our lives living in self-deceit!

Maestro: The highest of ironies indeed! For neither fish nor foul nor the gods themselves, need lie; that we are the lying animal can only mean that we alone are already 'open to' and 'standing in' the truth; that is, that we are the only place where truths are disclosed and can, therefore be dissimulated. It is no wonder then that from time to time we frail creatures fail our mission as guardians of the Truth as disclosure and fall from the weight of our responsibility into error and un-truth.

> *They all stop talking for a while, perplexed by what has just been said.*

---

13. We should keep in mind that when the Maestro uses the concept of 'Truth' with a capital 'T', he does not mean a Big Answer that would produce a dangerous ideology, but an ongoing and inexhaustible process of revealing Being. This process belongs to our essential being—the being who both discloses and conceals Being.

Paolo: Well, there is much to think about in what you say, I mean, about the usefulness of what appears useless,... and, well this way of thinking is difficult to get used to. But there is one other thing.

Maestro: What's that?

Paolo: The question about the gods—that we are reflections of the gods.

Maestro: Oh yes, about the gods. Did we not say that thinking, whether about the gods or anything else, is of its nature circular, that is, that no matter what we think or ask about, we do so only by assuming other ideas, which we are not thinking about at the time?

Paolo: Yes, and that it is the job of philosophy to question these assumptions and presupposed ideas, but about the gods...?

Maestro: That, my friend, is what I am getting to. When the Greeks invoked the names of their gods—when they thought about them—they did so from within the already assumed world of the gods; they could, therefore, only understand what the story of the gods allowed them to understand—whether about themselves or anything else. In other words, the Greeks did not create their gods but were rather born into the Olympian World.

Paolo: This I have trouble with. Don't you think someone had to invent them?

Maestro: And when someone creates or invents, does he do so out of nowhere, or does he create from his circumstances— from the ideas and materials available to him?

Paolo: Well,... the latter.

Maestro: So you see, Paolo, no man can be completely free of the historical epoch to which he is destined. It is from that particular place, and that unique time, with whatever limited view of the Truth he has, that man creates and invents—taking the past and present with him as he slowly pushes his horizon a bit further into the future.

Paolo: You are saying that when man creates his gods...

Maestro: Or any other belief for that matter-.

Paolo: He can only do so with the ideas that are available to him.

Maestro: Yes, from that part of the "Truth" which is revealed to him at that time and place.

Alessandro: Which is never the whole "Truth".

Maestro: No, only the part we are destined to, and in turn is destined to us.

Paolo: I think I see what you mean! What we think about, or how we understand ourselves, the world, or even the gods, is to some extent outside our control and conditioned by the circumstances we are born to. So when we think about our gods, we do so from what we already know about the gods.

Alessandro: And then we add to that our own situation—right?

Maestro: Exactly! Like all vital life, which of its nature must endure in the stream of time, we cannot return to a previous condition that is past, but must assume the circumstance that is ours in terms of a new situation and a future that is not yet. In this way, we are not only created beings—reflections of the gods—but also creators who must take what is given to us and re-form it in a way that speaks to our deepest concerns.

Paolo: And what concerned the Greeks was the problem of reason and instinct, order and chaos...

Alessandro: Apollo and Dionysus!

Maestro: Yes! Those names were used by the Greeks as a way to express how the Kosmos came to light for them—how its way of being was disclosed through their being, and how they in turn understood their being. Paolo was right; they understood and experienced their psyche—their soul—to be a place where a tremendous tension was felt between the One and Many, Being and Becoming, Time and Eternity and the Begining in the Beyond.

Alessandro: I think I feel it!

Maestro: Then you have been called to philosophy!

> *They all laugh aloud and stare for a*
> *moment at the dying embers.*

Maestro: But as you can see, our fire has gone out and I'm afraid it is time for us to part. Tomorrow you will both be leaving for good, to fulfill the destiny, which awaits you. I must stay awhile longer and wait for another season—another spring, which will, hopefully, bring with its blossoms some young men as fine as you Paolo... and you Alessandro.

> *They all rise and embrace each*
> *other.*

May the gods be with you.

Paolo: Maestro, I...

Alessandro: Will you write?

Maestro: Yes, to both of you.

LETTERS:

SIX VARIATIONS ON THE SAME THEME

VARIATION ONE

On the Sport of Dialectics

Dear Alessandro:

Greetings my friend, I received your letter and was pleased to hear that you were reading some of Plato's Dialogues. Do not be dismayed by your lack of understanding nor too impatient with our friend Socrates. Your frustration brings to mind my own when I first read the *Euthyphro*—the dialogue concerning the meaning of "piety." At last, I thought, I would draw some conclusions as to whether anything is sacred, or to put it in Socratic fashion, whether something is dear to the gods because it is good in-it-self, or good or holy because it is simply pleasing to the gods. And further, I expected I would understand something of man's relationship to God. I mean, it is certainly clear that we mortals stand much to gain from the gods, but what possibly could they need from us? Surely I would find some satisfaction here—some answer from one of the greatest philosophers. But by the end of the dialogue, just when I sensed I was nearing some conclusion, Socrates wound up back where he started. Needless to say, I felt discouraged but doggedly went on to another dialogue. This time it was *The Laches*—a conversation concerning the meaning of "courage." As you can surmise, the same thing happened again: first an opinion was given—as usual a most obvious and commonsensical opinion which Socrates easily found problematic; then another opinion a— one a bit more comprehensive—would be offered only to be followed by a further refutation, and so on. Each time it seemed that Socrates would lead his opponent in a circle with no adequate answer to the problem in question. I tried the next dialogue,...and the next. By Jove! I began to have some serious doubts about the whole business of Philosophy.

It wasn't until I read the *Republic* that I began to find some answers—this time a few too many answers. What I experienced was a kind of ambivalence of heart—a feeling of being both attracted by the beauty of systematic thought while at the same time repulsed by its stifling enclosure. It only occurred to me some years later that where the answers began, it was no longer Socrates speaking through the hand of Plato, but Plato; that is, it was no longer a recreation of a real conversation but a monologue parading as a dialogue. To be truthful, I think Plato, like the rest of the aristocratic Athenians, became annoyed with the Socratic method—fearful that its open ended and unresolved mode of inquiry was suited too well to the sophistic and democratic spirit of the times, and could by chance unleash the chaotic passions of anarchy. So it was that Plato succumbed to a certain temptation—the desire to create a more useful edifice: in short, a perfect state and final answer!

I just now used the word temptation. A curious word to use in regard to one who lived his life under the guidance of reason. I said Plato was tempted, but by whom or by what? Perhaps by the spirit of seriousness! By an over zealous love of truth and a certain proclivity to measure this truth in terms of mathematical certainty. But what great love! What noble love! To think, Alessandro, that it was Plato alone who tried to bring order and light to a place left dark and destitute by the departure of the Olympian gods—that it was he who struggled to create a new sense of justice and virtue amidst chaos and sophistry. It was Plato who brought the words of Socrates to life, and for this heroic effort a thousand generations owe him a debt of gratitude. No, there has been no greater intellectual courage nor love of truth. But never the less, Alessandro, the truth may be the greatest temptress of all. When we have 'the' truth on our side as our exclusive possession—as the 'only' truth—we inherit, along with the tremendous power it brings us, the danger of intellectual arrogance and unaccountability. I'm afraid that Plato, in his outrage over the execution of his master, and his disgust for the degenerate condition of Athens, grew weary of the sport of dialectics—he became serious! He could no longer allow common opinion and mob rule, with its endless and equivocal disputes, to reign as guardian over the destiny of Athens—even perhaps over the destiny of the West. And because he could no longer tolerate this thought, the youthful Plato girded his loins and went at the truth with the combination in his soul of the poet and the wrestler—he pinned her down! The game was over!

But Socrates knew better! We would do well to remember, Alessandro, when the Athenian citizens made their pilgrimage through the verdant hills of Hellas to the shrine of Apollo,—remember, and take to heart, that famous question they put to the oracle at Delphi concerning the wisest man in all of Athens. How strange and fitting that from deep inside the marble temple the clarion voice of a priestess should echo back the divine truth: "Socrates is the wisest man in all of Athens." What was it that Socrates knew that they didn't—that we still don't know? Here we must take care with the signs the gods give to man; they are much too rich in meaning to be taken literally or known unequivocally. I think the oracle could just as well have said, "Old Socrates knows women." I mean, suppose it is more the case, as one philosopher says (Nietzsche), that truth is a woman? If this were the case, then her seductive charm would not lie in her complete exposure as the truth, but in the way she elusively and capriciously changes her appearance precisely in order to keep hidden her mysterious nature. We, surely, would not want to restrict her to one appearance or make of her something practical—something one could manipulate, I would rather hope that we would answer her siren call with a response which does not violate her nature. Socrates knew this!

What Socrates knew, Alessandro, what his inner voice (*daimonion*) whispered to him and reminded him of, was that he must at all costs stay close to his nature and seek the truth, but never think he could know as a god knows—completely and finally. He must seek the truth with a thinking that always pauses and remains respectful before the profoundest of ideas—sacred ideas such as Truth, Beauty and Goodness, which of their nature must necessarily escape the total comprehension of we finite beings. Socrates knew that the truth of a profound idea—one that seeks to explain the fundamental ground of all things—would not reveal itself easily or directly but had to be approached in a roundabout way and be delicately delivered; and he also knew that the truth often hides behind what appears as obvious and common place; so instead of clutching tenaciously and covetously at one aspect of the truth—one accepted disclosure, and just one lovely appearance—Socrates would allow the object of his inquiry to show itself in a preliminary way in its first appearance 'as' a truth; then with care, he would show how this common and taken for granted view of the truth (*doxa*)—this common opinion—contained much confusion and ambiguity; he did this by showing how the first opinion (A), if pushed too far, would yield a contradiction (-A); he would show, for instance, how an unthoughtful definition of justice, if strictly followed, could lead to a case of injustice. By doing this, Socrates was better able to coax the truth from her hiding place so she could shyly show herself in another form—a form from which a new opinion could be derived (B); this time it would be an opinion which would be a synthesis and expansion of the first two opposing ones, and would, therefore, be a more comprehensive and more knowledgeable opinion. It is in this way, Alessandro—the dialectical way which takes apart in order to preserve and rebuild—that thinking gives substance to the psyche. And as you know, he would not stop with a new opinion. No, he would stay on track and do the same thing again, each time seeing the object of his inquiry from an necessarily higher and consequently more comprehensive and beautiful view—one which surveys and remembers all the incomplete deficient opinions below, but never all the possible ones above. Socrates remained open to the truth by being careful of its nature and of his own ignorance—careful, that is, not to be tempted by the spirit of seriousness into thinking he could attain 'the' truth. Socrates knew this! And the gods were pleased.

The "art" of thinking, and it is an art which must like all arts be worked on and mastered, lies not in the mere collection of information and facts, nor in the various logical 'techniques' of clarity and symbolic control, but must like all other art forms first presuppose that which makes it an art—the art of love. The knowledge and practice of this art will insure that the object of our concern, whatever that may be, will be given its proper care and 'respect': when we love, and love truly, what we love will be released from the bondage of our self-interest and coercion and allowed to be what it is in its own way of being. In this way, the integrity of what is 'other' than ourselves is preserved and kept safe. When, for instance, the artist works on his material, he must take this material as he finds it and be guided by its intrinsic nature. If he is not sensitive and caring about that which he works on, no art can emerge. And when we think, Alessandro, should we not also take care and pay heed to the matter of our thought—to the life of the idea we are thinking about? And should we not follow this idea where it points, and see what other ideas it relates to?

You see, most ideas are not created by us but are found in the world much like the artifacts that are found in an archaeological site. They come to us already worked on by other artists in other times, with a story of their own to tell. When we look at some ancient vase, what we find are images and reflections of a certain tradition, which has been covered over by layers of sedimentation. And if we are to fully appreciate this vase, we would best handle it with care and listen closely to what it may have to say about its world—about where it has been, and what it has meant to others. If we do so, Alessandro, we will see that the vase will implicate many things beyond itself: it will first of all point back to the life of the man who painstakingly crafted it; but for what purpose was it created? Was this vase filled with grain and stored for the winter months, or did it carry wine to some sacrificial alter on the highest of holidays? From around this one vase a multitude of questions and possible answers will radiate forth, each revealing a different dimension of the life-world from which the vase arose; and with each question we ask of it, Alessandro, we, ourselves, will be put in question. How are our problems different? What gods do we believe in? And why have we no sacrificial altars? We can only find out something if we ask a question, and we can only ask a question if we ourselves are beings who are in some way questionable—that is—if we ourselves are not sure of who or what we are. So with each question we ask of some other thing or person, we learn more about ourself—perhaps, more about what we don't know about ourselves!

And so it is with a good idea! It comes to us already loaded down with other meanings from other times, within a web of relations; if we are to recover the truth of this idea, we must first pause before it in a moment of silence and wonder... as before a rare find; then we must question it in a way which allows it to unveil itself; and every new meaning we find—every possible new answer—will turn back on us as a question. But when we enter into such a dialogue with an idea, we should do so without losing track or doing violence to the single line of thought we are pursuing—the single thread which binds together the various meanings that constitute the life and integrity of the idea. And if our inquiry comes to a dead end, if, that is, we cannot find some final meaning to attach to the mystery of the vase, it would be best if we put it back in some cool, dark place where perhaps someone else, in some other time, may stumble across it and see it anew. But we ourselves, must continue to search and move on to other ideas and other meanings.

Now that I look back on it, Alessandro, the secret to Socratic wisdom was right before my very eyes. What Socrates taught, in his own way, was to remain faithful—to never let a final answer or accomplished goal keep us from our search. The answer I was looking for, Alessandro, was to be found in the 'way' taken—a way which stays open to the 'truth' as a process of disclosure. The answer is precisely found in the search itself! This does not mean that we can hold no opinion; that would surely be contrary to our nature; it does mean, however, that we should struggle to give our opinion 'substance' and so make it worthy of consideration and always open to the possibility of error.

So, do not be discouraged or perplexed when Socrates takes you from one definition to another, dissecting and synthesizing, moving around like an artful boxer with his shadow, always ready, if need be, to strike a loving blow against the more hardened crust of untruth. This is simply his way of turning opinion into knowledge. His method—the dialectical method—is the gift that Socrates bequeathed to mankind. It is the means by which the truth is set free and we become free for the truth. His legacy is the highest and noblest of sports because it is the one, which listens to our deepest concerns and, therefore, stays close to our essential nature as guardians of the truth. This sport is to the mind what music is to the heart—what gymnastics is to the body—it makes the sinews of the soul more subtle and magnanimous. Be of great heart Alessandro!

Con amore,
Maestro

P.S. I am going to make a copy of this letter so as not to repeat myself. Forgive me if I am sometimes forgetful.

VARIATION TWO

On One's True Vocation

Dear Alessandro,

I am always happy to hear from you and to learn what new and interesting things you are doing. You did, however, express some concern over what you are ultimately to do with yourself—what, that is, your vocation in life should be. You asked how one could know what path to follow, especially when life seems to invite us in so many possible directions. I must say that I am not at all sure I am qualified to help you in this regard; but if I do feel compelled to try, it is because I have had a great deal of time to be foolish and have often been errant in my ways. And what more can a teacher and a friend possibly be than a good guide who at least knows which paths not to take? But do not expect, Alessandro, that I have anything at all specific to tell you—that I will direct you to this job or that. I must answer, as I usually do in keeping with my vocation, which is to think, and talk only of 'things in general' and nothing in particular.

First, we should pay close attention to what the word 'vocation' says. We often confuse this word with "doing" some kind of work. But the word 'vocation' speaks about the 'call' to work, if we mean by work, not just any work, but that activity which is best suited to us. What is really in question here, Alessandro, is one's "true vocation"—meaning that which calls upon us to be most fully ourselves. And as you know, this must necessarily differ with each individual. The "Principle of Identity," which states that one thing is the same as another, can never apply to that which endures in the flow of time—to that which lives; no two sentient beings can experience life in exactly the same way, at the same time and place, but must of necessity reflect their own unique perspective on the world; and yet,... there is in all things which differ something which remains the same—a unity in difference, if you like. Do we not share a commonplace and fate with even the smallest of creatures, and perhaps even with what we might mistakenly call the inorganic? We toil, we eat, we rest, but above all, we struggle like all things to persist each in our own way of being; and does not this word 'being', which we rightly apply to each thing which 'is', also point to that which is our common ground— 'Being' itself? I mean, because we all 'are' in some way, what we all share is precisely this process of 'Being'. So, one's "true vocation" must not only beckon forth that which is most individual in us, but must also reverberate in its call a universal principle, which like a silent and invisible wave runs through all things, connecting man to man, and all to all. But this I would prefer to speak of later; for now, we should return to the word 'vocation' which we have delineated in a preliminary fashion as a 'call'. But who or what is it that calls to us?

What if I were to tell you, dear Alessandro, that it is our destiny that calls to us and patiently awaits our arrival? What would you say? Would you say this meant that we are not free— that like particles in motion we are determined by the laws of causality to complete our fated course? And if this is so, why then should we concern ourselves with a future that will take care of itself? But how strange, indeed, that we can even be "concerned about" or aware of a future! Just think, Alessandro, we are a kind of thing which not only wonders about its future and what will become of itself, but questions its own being as a thing. We are strange things indeed, who in questioning our own thingly character transcend mere thinglyness! Strictly speaking, Alessandro, other things cannot have a future at all!—they are always caught in the constant now. It could even be argued that that which has no future can neither have a past nor a present; what could it possibly mean for a rock, or a plant, or even a higher animal to weigh its past and be concerned about its future? The future of a mere thing can only mean another condition at some other point in space which is necessarily dictated by the previous causes and conditions external to the thing itself. You might say that things are always pushed from behind and remain unaware of their options.

But to have a future is something different: it means that our present is both haunted by the ghost of what 'was' and the specter of what 'will be'; it means that we must suffer the melancholy and despair over what is necessary and 'past', and endure the anxiety of what is possible and 'not yet'. But tell me, Alessandro, when we reach the next moment or even tomorrow, will we reach our future? I think not! The future is not another point down the line, but is rather more like the horizon we see in the distance which always stays one step ahead of us and can never be caught; but unlike the real place outside where the sun sets behind the mountains and forever recedes as we approach, the future is more like an "internal horizon" which intimately belongs to us as a lived experience. Although we can never completely catch or consummate our future, we are bound to it as a living possibility. It would appear then, that since we do not have a future in exactly the same way as other things, we could neither be determined in precisely the same manner. An 'actual thing' is necessarily enslaved by its immediate conditions and responds accordingly; but we, Alessandro, we are "possible things" who can turn the dead inertia of our environment into a field of possibilities to choose from. Because we are one step ahead of the past and off into the emptiness of the future, we are free to turn our glance back upon the world and decide what we will do. But you ask, how can the future, which is empty and "not yet", call to us as our destiny?

You see, Alessandro, we are surely a thing like all other things—a fact in the world—subject like they are to the concrete and factual conditions that surround us and ceaselessly push us from behind, but we are also drawn by the very possibilities we are able to project ahead of ourselves. Because we are a peculiar thing that is outside and ahead of itself in time—towards its future—we are a 'possible thing', and can, therefore, look at ourselves and wonder what we will be. It does sound queer, but only that which is outside of itself ("out of its head," as you once said), can possibly see in some vague way where it is going. So what calls to us, as our destiny is none other than our own possible self that calls to us from a place in the future where our ideal self both awaits us and eludes our capture.

In plainer language, Alessandro, knowing our "true vocation" has to do with paying close attention to our circumstances—to our limitations as to what we can do and listening carefully to what our real possibilities are. All things are possible, its true, but not "authentically" so. What is authentic for us is what can be accomplished now, with these particular talents, in this time span allotted to us, within and against the cultural-historical environment we inherit. We cannot for a moment pretend we are someone else in some other place and time; another time will have its own frame of reference—its own way of responding to and disclosing its world, and its own rendezvous with destiny. I often say, Alessandro, that growing up has much to do with elimination of these inauthentic possibilities, and growing old with grace depends heavily on the courageous acceptance of the one possibility left.

Each of us, then, has a particular vocation, unique unto ourselves, which results from the tension and play between what for us is necessarily determined and past, and that which is still possible in the future. These two things—the "necessary" and the"possible"—are the Scylla and Charybdis of our existence. Through these straights we must continually pass without being swept away by either current; if we lose courage and veer off course, we will either succumb to necessity and run aground in shallow and stagnant waters, or be drawn out to sea to slowly drown in possibilities. In the first case we say, "I can do nothing," and in the second one says, "I can do everything." Be careful, Alessandro, of both these dangers.

But as I said before, if it is to be a "true vocation," it will also reflect that which is universal in all things and calls to us in a larger voice. It is this call that reminds us that we are all rooted in and nourished by the same ground—that we are all beings in Being. And if we do not hearken to that which constitutes our greater self—to the call of Being—we will surely wither away and fall from our most authentic possibility. But the question now remains as to how we can know and be sure that our vocation will be a "true vocation" and, thereby, answer properly to the call of Being. I'm afraid that on this question we must proceed with much trepidation. For when we reach the crucial point—the point where our need for decision and commitment intersects our abstract life—all dialectical play and philosophical debate must stop and an act of fidelity must begin. At this juncture we have only our deepest feelings to navigate by and the testimony of those sages we most respect that stand like fixed stars in the constellations of the past.

The most I can tell you Alessandro, from what little I have learned, is that unless your vocation stays near to what is either of the True, the Beautiful, or the Good, it will not touch what is most universal: if you listen carefully, and remove yourself from the sound and fury of that which surrounds you, you will hear at least one of these call to you; they are the three faces of Being which reveal to man what is most universal; and to each of these belongs an appropriate response: I, myself, have been called to but one face of Being—to the study of philosophy which must respond, like science and mathematics, by thinking the "truth" of Being; others cultivate their aesthetic sensitivities through the discipline of one art or another, and so dwell in close proximity to the Beautiful; and still others respond to the Good by living a life of devotion and care. I have always hoped that if I looked long enough, and deeply enough into any one face, I might catch a glimpse of the other two. Now, I can't describe with much precision the nature of the three things about which I speak, nor give any guarantee for what must remain only intimations of Being; but if apart from whatever particular thing you do in life, you also learn to 'think' honestly and clearly, 'feel' and appreciate what is harmonious, and 'act' with both courage and kindness towards all things—if you do at least one of these, dear Alessandro, you will touch what is common to all and binds each to each.

Goodbye, caro mio, and keep course!

Maestro

VARIATION THREE

On Freedom and Philosophy

Dear Alessandro,

I received your letter the other morning just as I was leaving for the most southerly section of the orchard; having no time to read it at that moment, I tucked it away in my pack with my bread and drink and carried it with me while I worked among the trees. Later in the day, when the sun moved directly overhead and I could feel the drops of moisture collect upon my brow, I stopped my work and sat in the shade—beneath the old elm. When I opened your letter, the words I read began to mingle with the taste of summer wine and the smell of damp, newly irrigated earth— they mixed in such a way so as to call forth many images and memories of our time together. I must say, Alessandro, that with each letter I receive, I find your questions furrowing into deeper ground and your thoughts beginning to ripen. Perhaps they will one day drop in fullness and in turn bear fruit of their own. And so it appears, my boy, that Heraclitus was right about the reality of change; for as the seasons come and go, you are growing in every way, and I am shrinking and slowing down; it is even rumored that this beautiful orchard, so fragrant and abundant with wild life, will soon be ploughed under and leveled out. So, if you do not hear from me for a while, I will be going elsewhere in search of some way to be useful.

Now, the question as to what work is most useful to us is of great importance; for what is most useful to man must surely be what most effectively makes him man—what, that is, cultivates that which belongs to man as uniquely his own. And man as we discussed before, is not merely an actual being but a "possible being" who must not only reflect upon ideas, but must also reflect upon himself and decide what he will do or what he will be. What belongs to man, Alessandro, as being what is most uniquely his own, is nothing less than the possibility for taking some measure of control over who he is. What is most useful to us, then, is what helps to cultivate and develop the self as the responsible self that it can become; and a responsible self must, by definition, be a free self. So, I would say that the work which is most useful to man is the 'work of freedom'—the work which frees the self for its own possibility. We must not, however, confuse the work of becoming free with the work of doing nothing, which, by the way, is mistakenly thought to be no work at all; on the contrary, some of us have spent a great deal of time and energy on being diligent and crafty in the sublime art of idleness; nor should we confuse being too industrious with the work of freedom. On the one hand, we have the work of the lazy, and on the other, we have the work of the busy—but in neither case do we have the work of freedom. Rather, what we have is the work which is most proper for cultivating one's self as an "actual thing"—the work of slavery!

When we do the work of slavery, we are more useful to others than to ourselves, and so confuse what is most useful to us with being used. Let me explain: if I am lazy in both mind and body, I will soon be overtaken by an environment gone out of my control; the responsibilities I secretly avoid will soon encroach upon me and hold me captive—like a prisoner; I will only be able to run, or live forever in a place run by others. This, Alessandro, is life in flight—not freedom! If, on the other hand, I become industrious and truly believe that money and the material goods it brings can totally buy my freedom, I will sooner or later find myself in a debtors prison of the heart—held captive by my own greed and the captains of capital who pull the invisible strings by which I dangle; and if, per chance, I work hard enough at becoming wealthy, and am able to control some of the strings myself, then I will grow increasingly dependent on the puppets who sustain my show. This is high comedy, Alessandro, that the puppeteer should sleep with one eye open in fear of a puppet revolt! That is how we confuse the work of freedom with the work most proper to slavery. Being used, you see, belongs to the nature of actual things, and not to we possible beings; to enslave a possible being—a free being—is to corrupt and abuse what is most natural to it by turning it into an object. And even with actual things—trees, plants and animals, which have no responsibility for their lives—even here, we must be careful to use them in ways which correspond to and respect their nature and, in many cases, their likeness to us in suffering disease and death.

What I am getting at, Alessandro, is the notion that there is a kind of work which will, if pushed too far, demean and enslave the human self by making a thing of it, and one which will set it free for becoming what it most truly is—a possibility. We saw that both working at nothing and working too much will ultimately fail,—unless, of course, one prefers to be a slave. Perhaps, then, we must learn to work at doing whatever we want? That must surely be what we are looking for! Wouldn't it be grand, Alessandro, to follow every inclination we feel, pursue every possibility, and satiate every desire? Wouldn't it be fun to never settle long in any one place, and always move on to something else when bored: to always be on the lookout for what is new and interesting, but never look too deeply into anything? Perhaps we should continually buzz around like a bee from flower to flower, first tasting, then robbing each one of its nectar? Is this not the work best suited to we possible beings? Oh! If only we were more like bees! At least for every grain of pollen they carry away there will be a drop of honey. But what is it that doing whatever we want really brings?

What we have here, Alessandro, is but another sort of slavery. This time however, it is the slavery of a chaotic heart, which swirls in possibilities, and takes and takes, but never produces anything of substance in return. When doing only what we want, we become helplessly addicted to our own pleasures and inclinations which voraciously consume everything around leaving only a craving and vacuous self behind. I do not mean to say, however, that the work of freedom must produce an external and tangible result. No, being totally pragmatic in this way would bring us closer to what is most animal in us and further from what is essentially human: the animal is perfectly practical and does nothing which does not in some way suit his needs for survival. We, of course, must have our external needs met—they are surely necessary conditions for our well being; but, Alessandro, they are not sufficient. I mean, they are not enough for the survival of what is most essentially human. What good is a rising standard of living—quantitative increase of the bigger, smaller, and faster — and the liberties and rights that go with it, if we remain enslaved to ourselves? I tell you, my friend that these luxuries and freedoms are dangerous without a change of heart and mind. What the work of freedom must produce is an internal transformation—a transformation without which the self will stagnate and die. It must be the work, which helps free the self from the bondage of its own enslaved state of being; it is the work that enhances the mastery of the self over the 'subject' created by others.

You are probably wondering at this point how it is that the self is not master of its own subjectivity. To what is it enslaved? Well, when we go in search of this self of ours to see precisely how it comes into being, we will see that it is originally 'thrown' quite helplessly into an environment it did not create and hardly comprehends: from the most sublime regions of infinite space and time to the most ordinary and finite objects, we have but the slightest understanding; we find ourselves in the humiliating condition of being caught between, and at the mercy of, the forces of nature, society, technology, history, our body, and even the most common things around us. It is no wonder, then, that what we understand as "our" self is, at first, not ours at all, but constituted and controlled by what is outside of it. So, when the self finally begins to rub its eyes and ask who and what it is, it answers with a curious assortment of ideas: it says it is a "soul", a "body," a "mind," a "biochemical organism," a "calculating mechanism," a "child of God," or a "person with inalienable rights." What we find when we go in search of the self is not a thing at all, but a process of interpretation, explanation, and self-justification. What we find, in short, is the self as a concocted abstract entity.

Now, where, pray tell, does one get such notions about one's self? Why, from a variety of sources: friends, relatives, parents, tradition, mythology, religious authority, gossip, newspapers, magazines, certain easily digestible books,—all, for the most part, acquired in a relatively passive way from sources outside ourselves which we accept or reject in accordance with our feelings and inclinations. And to think, Alessandro, that it is on such flimsy grounds as these, using ideas which do not belong to us, that we not only form our concepts of ourselves and the world, but loudly proclaim our opinions on the profoundest of matters. Yes, we even decide on questions of life and death, and happily pass the hemlock to those opposed to our view of things. I tell you, never before have men talked so much about so many things and have said so little! We have all but forgotten, Alessandro, that the lover of opinion—the "philodoxer"—once designated the oppositional character to the "philosopher" as the lover of wisdom. How strange that we now find ourselves on the other side of the battle for the soul.

But we should not be too harsh on ourselves, for this desire and capacity to form an opinion and have a point of view is the first quickening which heralds the birth of philosophical self as it tries to struggle free from the cocoon of its enslaved subjectivity. Yet, this 'point of view' of ours is not what we mean by a knowledgeable opinion nor a fully developed understanding. As soon as we recognize that we have been seduced, captured and manipulated by someone else's ideas—that we are not free at all— as soon as we become aware of this condition of servitude, we can begin the work of freedom; and that, as you have probably already guessed, is the work of philosophy as the care of self.

How is it, then, that philosophy helps the self gain mastery over its own self? We will find a clue to this work if we first ask how one masters anything. What, for instance, does the craftsman do, or the artist, or the musician, in order to gain mastery over his own particular craft? Contrary to current educational 'methodologies', learning does not take place merely with the back and forth putatively equal opinions, nor in the expression and argumentative defense of one's already acquired skills and thinking patterns, but rather—as Descartes showed—with the temporary suspension of ones everyday convictions and practices. If we take notice, it will be obvious that each instance of true creativity and craftsmanship entails a great deal of discipline: the woodcarver or furniture builder must learn, through a long period

102

of apprenticeship, to use his tools properly and understand the nature of the wood with which he works; and the more the artist understands the materials, colors, and techniques with which he works—the more, that is, he trains his eyes to see—the more freedom he gains to create as he pleases; but nowhere is this more apparent than with the improvisational techniques of both classical and modern music: in order for the musician to freely create on his instrument, he must first master and control all the various scales and rhythmical nuances of meter. Then, and only then, will the fingers of his body and the feelings and conceptions of his mind fuse in the free flight of creativity. This kind of freedom is far removed from the so-called freedom of doing what we want! The freedom of creativity and master craftsmanship is won only from self-imposed discipline. It is, my friend, as Nietzsche tells us, to "dance in chains." But what exactly are these chains the self must overcome and master?

What the self is chained to, *caro mio*, is ironically its own view of things. We are trapped and controlled by the very picture we construct in order to understand ourselves and the world. Because this picture is, as we saw, constructed from the hodgepodge and ragtag of ideas around us, it is inevitable that this borrowed perspective will dictate what and how we see in a way which is not our own and often contradictory. This is the externally created 'subject' which the reflective and possible self must keep an eye on. What we want—better, what we need—is our 'own' coherent point of view! You are now probably thinking that there is some contradiction in all this—that it's all subjective. But this is clearly not the case. What I would like to say, Alessandro, is that the work of philosophy does not require that we create a new idea or hold an original point of view; even if this were possible, a novel idea is not necessarily a philosophical one! What the craft of philosophy does require is that we make this or that point of view our own by way of re-appropriating that which we have already used but is still outside of ourselves and out of our understanding and control. To appropriate something means to take it into ourselves; but to reappropriate something means to take in, work on it, and then and make it our own: just as the earthworm must take in the dirt around it and metabolize it into its own cellular structure, and the leaf must drink up the sunlight to do its job and produce the fruit of the tree, so too, does the self take in and appropriate the environment proper to it. And the self, as we saw, most truly belongs to the world of ideas and images which it uses to know itself and the world; but as we also saw, the self uses and appropriates what is still not its own: Although all living things are involved in an act of appropriation, and truly belong to their environment, we, Alessandro, are essentially dispossessed. What seems to be given to man alone is the curious task of making what belongs to him his own. We must not only take in and consume ideas, but must chew and digest them before they can be synthesized and emerge once again as a point of view; this time, however, they will be re-appropriated and transformed into our own point of view. This act of re-appropriation is the discipline most proper to the craft and work of philosophy. It is the action whereby the self subjects its self and the ideas it holds to a critical examination and thereby comes into possession of its self.

And so it is, my friend, that we do the work of freedom by becoming masters over the various ideas that surround us and would otherwise enslave us. This is the work most proper to philosophy—the work that not only attempts to free us from the tyranny of nature and the despotism of other ideologies, but struggles to free us from the autocratic rule of the inauthentic and unconscious self over the responsible self which is still possible.

Maestro

Postscript:
There is one more thing I would like to say concerning the freedom that the work of philosophy brings—a warning, if you will permit me. Once we have learned the critical art of dissecting and relating ideas—once, that is, we become accustomed to the freedom of "philosophical detachment"—we may begin to enjoy the safety of being "uncommitted." We may now flit about, not from one

pleasure to another, but from one point of view to another, cynically showing the faults, contradictions and imperfections intrinsic to them all. But this kind of hit and run tactic is no great feat! It hides not only a lack of integrity, which comes from a disunified self, but also a great deal of intellectual cowardice. A point of view which aspires to be truly philosophical requires the courage to avoid both the security of "dogmatism" and the smugness of "cynicism" by taking upon itself the responsibility of giving back a better point of view than the one it destroys; and this new view must be committed to only in what Kierkegaard called..."fear and trembling."

VARIATION FOUR

On the Impractical and Uncommonsensical

Paolo, my friend,

    I, too, miss our conversations and am sorry to have left so many thoughts in disarray when last we parted. I am feeling well, but I must confess that I am moving through the trees a bit slower and doing my work with less enthusiasm these days. What I need is another good apprentice like you who will interrupt me from time to time with an interesting question or two. I think that is exactly what I need! Yes, a good question—one which will open up a region in which to think: an "unreal" place to go where I can slowly wander about and find some rest and respite from the tedium of my daily chores. I do remember, however, that you found some difficulty in understanding the relevancy of the kind of thinking I most enjoy. But it does occur to me, Paolo, that the origin of thinking itself must have something to do with what is in a certain sense irrelevant and impractical; it must have something to do with the capacity of ours to explore worlds. And it also seems clear that this capacity is dependent on the growth and development of imagination, which cannot occur without some leisure time. I mean, if we are busy hunting and gathering, we certainly have no need nor time to wonder about or question anything—we must simply survive. But as soon as we have enough to satisfy our basic needs—just as soon as life becomes abundant—we begin to look at our very same surroundings in a different way: we no longer say, "give me" or "I need," but "what if;" that is, we no longer look at our circumstances for what they are, but beyond them to what they can be; we no longer rest content with our cold cave walls but begin to adorn them with the delicate lines of the wildebeest.

    It is abundance and the leisure time it brings which not only make possible the world of hypothetical speculation, but also the world of play. Contrary to what we are taught about need being the mother of invention, it is from plenitude and free time that both thinking and play spring forth. And these two things are not as far apart as we seem to think, but share a common source—boredom! This seems a most unlikely clue to what could be most central to human existence, but as the poet sings: it is here "in the fowl rag and bone shop of the heart" where all such inquiry must start.[14] The fact is, we are creatures who get bored! Oh, our animal friends do indeed fret about and sulk, but are usually content when the object of their need has been met. But we, Paolo, are just the opposite! It is precisely when our material needs are met that our discontent begins. We find ourselves in the curious position of having "time on our hands." I say curious because to have "time on one's hands" means that we are never quite in the present but in a continual state of anticipation. This is what I meant when I said some time ago that we are not ourselves in some way. Boredom provides a clue to our nature—our nature as temporal beings. It points to the fact that we are a kind of being who at every moment is also beyond the moment toward the future. You see, Paolo, if we were destined to be only in the present, we could not get bored and would, in the strictest sense of the word, be quite practical, that is, we would do only those things that were beneficial to our immediate condition. But we are in the present always by way of worrying about some future condition—some imaginary possibility. We are not immediate at all, but always off someplace else in a perpetual kind of daydream. What is most practical for man—and that means what is best suited to his nature—is that he be able to free himself from the confines of his immediate environment and fly off into the imaginary world of thought. And, hopefully, with every return flight a new dimension will be superimposed over his old world in order to transform it into something which suits his new but restless needs. It seems that what we consider at the moment to be the most practical of necessities—houses, transportation, tools, etc.—are all things which were once the twinkle in the eye of a man with some "time on his hands;" and these things in turn will soon be supplanted by our own discontent. What I am clumsily trying to say, Paolo, is that at the heart of what we call the "practical" lies a hidden but fundamental kind of "impracticality"—a kind of impracticality

14. From the Poem, "The Circus Animals' Desertion," *Last Poems,* 1939 by William Butler Yeats

which belongs essentially to the restlessness of the human spirit which must always take off and return.

There is a story you might have heard about the father of philosophy, Thales, who, while stargazing with his head in the clouds, fell into a ditch. It must have been an never ending source of amusement to the villagers to see such behavior and to near such uncommonsensical ideas flow from he mouth of this obscure fellow. You can imagine what they thought upon hearing that the stars were made of fire and earth; and that all things were fundamentally water; or that the earth was a spherical ball thousands of miles around. I'm sure they began to talk unkindly about this unusual and uncommonsensical man. Well, it seems that Thales became irritated with all the clamor and decided to put his knowledge of the stars and the seasons to some practical use. The story has it that because he was able to predict a bountiful olive harvest and buy up all the pressing mechanisms before hand, he became quite wealthy. Now, whether this is true or not, it doesn't take much imagination to see that what is often born of the impractical—in this case a kind of abstract thinking—can have not only useful consequences, but can also be very dangerous. We need only think of how strange it must have sounded when Democritus said that what one actually sees before one's very eyes is not really what it appears to be, but is rather made up of invisible particles called atoms? we need only think of this and then notice what consequence will soon come from this abstraction! You see, Paolo, it is the paradoxical nature of thinking, especially philosophical thinking which attempts to know the whole, to remain to a large degree abstract; it cannot rest content with hearsay and what seems to be the case, but must temporarily step away from what is most ordinary and commonsensical precisely in order to better see what is really there. The Egyptians were master builders and, of course, 'used' the plumb-line; but when Euclid 'defined' the line and other geometric objects, the mind became liberated from the limits of the material world and entered the theoretical domain. Thinking, if it is to remain true to its reflective nature, must courageously sacrifice itself before the altar of ridicule and common opinion and temporarily enter the realm of the imaginary and abstract; then and only then, Paolo, can thinking return and win back in a new way what is most concrete. So it is only natural that the comic poet Aristophanes would lower Socrates on the stage in a basket and have him say amidst the laughter of the audience, "I walk on air and contemplate the sun."

Frankly, Paolo, it is difficult not to be annoyed when people persist in thinking in certain ruts about philosophy and its impracticality. Perhaps they believe that we can do without it! But how can we possibly fail to notice that man will give up food and water—the most practical of necessities—and lay down his life for some abstract idea about what he considers to be most "real" or most "just," or a matter of his "rights;" how can we fail to see that above the hard crust of the earth there floats another more ephemeral encompassing—a second nature of ideas which constitutes the so called unreal medium from which the life of the human spirit must draw its breath. This, once again, is not an actual place of hardened facts, but a counterfactual domain where ideas, laws, hopes and dreams dwell. No, I'm afraid we cannot do without this inclination of ours for rarefied air—this superfluous need to venture forth into unknown regions and imaginary worlds; we cannot do without a little nonsense, a dash of color, a new sound, a thought, a belief—especially a philosophy of some sort. In fact, Paolo, you might say that man is not so much another "thing-in-the-world" as much as he is a "point-of-view-on-the-world"—a view surveyed from the height of a basket hovering a few feet above reality. What we seem to continually need is a better look—a little stretch of the neck to see where we are. And so it is that we cannot let well enough alone, but seem comically condemned to justify our existence: to make up reasons and live by some view of reality and to have one foot in a basket and one on the ground. If we feel no need to examine our ideas and assumptions, that is, to do philosophy, I'm afraid we have no other choice but to be swept along by the values and beliefs of others. One way or the other, Paolo, there is no escape from philosophy! We can only do it in a better or worse way.

The question then is not how to extricate ourselves from this impractical philosophical predicament, but how to plunge deeper into, and thereby stay closer to the core of our nature. Human nature consists essentially, and for the most part, in its quest to know its condition. Put another way, it is of our essence to be problematic: to question, to wonder, and to be philosophical! This we cannot rid ourselves of without also ridding ourselves of our essential humanity. We can only hope to indulge in that which belongs to us with some measure of honesty and courage. What is at stake is nothing less than the freedom and integrity that is gained by a thinking which asks about "who," "what," and "where" we are. But now, Paolo, I must come down from my basket, as we all must do, and return to the market place.

Maestro

VARIATION FIVE

On Science and Philosophy

Dear Paolo,

I'm glad to hear you are doing well at school but I am not at all surprised that you have left your study of the Law and have become enamored of the Natural Sciences. A good critical mind, such as yours, will always be drawn to those disciplines that seek to master the equivocal and ambiguous elements of life. You did, however, remind me once again about the essential difference between science and philosophy. You quite agreed that science has its moments of impracticality, and of course must use certain abstractions, but, you said, it always "returns" to the real world and puts its findings to the test. Philosophy, on the other hand, never seems to touch ground in quite the same way. This is correct—but deserves no apology! What appears at first sight to be an intrinsic weakness is also the heart and strength of philosophy. Now, if you will allow me, Paolo, I would like to remind you of something. I would like to remind you that philosophy, which for centuries has been called the "Queen of the Sciences" is quite proud of its most successful but often arrogant offspring. Like any good parent, she must suffer the humiliation of being surpassed by the strength and beauty of youth, yet waits with patience for the return of her prodigal and thankless prince—waits with the patience and confidence of one who has weathered the seasons and vicissitudes of life.

Now, since all things are necessarily connected, and so will inevitably seek the source from which they first sprang, we would do well, Paolo, to remember the beginning of philosophy, and how those first Mediterranean thinkers took their stand in the clear light of day and raised their questions to heaven itself. And they should rightly be called philosophers, not merely because they freed themselves from the tyranny of the Gods, but because they wanted to know, just for the sake of knowing; to think independently and look and see for themselves; but most of all, they deserve this title for their enduring and unending search for the answer to the question of the "One and the Many"—to the flow of becoming and the question of Being. We should not forget that it is from this primal experience of wonder about all there is that the various "specific" areas of inquiry were born. When science remembers the mystery and wonder from which it originates, and attempts to infuse this feeling into its research and findings, it becomes true science. If it does not, if, that is, it is forgetful of the underground spring from which it derives its vitality—if it persists in trying to be the last word by reducing all forms of thought to its own method,—if it does this, it is in danger of falling into what Vico called a "Second Barbarism," or what today is called scientism or positivism.

As you can see, I would like to maintain a certain distinction between "science" and "scientism." Only those who participate in the former discipline are the true heirs of philosophy with whom we have none but a lovers' quarrel. But over and against those who hold to the latter view, we must keep a constant vigil, and treat them in the same way as we would those who hold to any dogma, ideology, or incivility. I'm sure, Paolo, you are familiar with the modern attitude of "scientism"—the attitude of those who have become drunk with technological power and seek in one continuous orgy to control, manipulate, and reverse engineer everything in sight. I'm sure you have heard them going from village to village shouting their paean:

Come out! Come out! You have nothing to fear,
for the past is dead and the future is here.
Life is a puzzle which can be solved.
Come out! Come out! And be absolved.

Beware of these zealots, Paolo, they have sacrificed their first-born to Apollo and have stayed too long in the sun. They now suffer a peculiar disease, which accrues from too much of a good thing—false infinitude: too much transparency, too much information, too much faith in progress, too much control, and above all, too much practical success. They are suffering from the dizziness of mental heat prostration and can no longer see where they are, nor remember anything of the past. Everywhere they only see their own reflection! What else can one mean by "barbarism" Paolo, but the kind of historical forgetfulness which leads to myopic use and abuse of everything close at hand—a nearsightedness which uses nature without care and gives no thanks, nor acknowledgment, to the thousands of backs on which science and civilization stand. And while being oblivious to the past, these ingenuous devotees of "scientism"—these intellectual nomads who wander from project to project—happily promise to make our future life more humane through the use of their method and its creations. But when anything is created apart from the larger questions concerning the good of man and his destiny, that is, apart from what is essentially most humane, then the **means** will have been mistaken for the **end**—the created thing for the process of creation. When this happens, Paolo, that which is created by the hand of man will almost always turn against man in the most monstrous and inhumane ways.

And so with every new invention of this kind which promises to make life and learning faster and easier for everyone,—with every new gadget which promises to bring man closer to man—we ironically become more alienated from ourselves and others: alone and surrounded by a world filled with technological "things" and the superficial modes of communication they engender, we, like ducklings imprinting on mother duck, begin to see ourselves as reflections of the "things" which surround us; following their lead, we begin to confuse the swapping of topical "information" with dialogue, "calculation" with thoughtfulness , and "manipulation" is mistaken for authentic encounter; without wonder, the world is seen merely as a puzzle with missing parts; the other becomes a number to be filed in a statistical column; and we ourselves? Well, behold!—Man the Gadget! Beware, Paolo, of those who come bearing such gifts but know no Greek; they are modern fellows who have been claimed by the "spirit of reductionism" and see only through the eyes of their own specialty;—about them, we must remain critical! Without wonder and love (*philia*), they act as inquisitors of nature and are pretenders to the throne!

But as to those true scientists who remain the rightful heirs of philosophy, to them we owe our deepest respect and gratitude. They have always gone about the business of discerning and ferreting out the secrets of nature with the utmost humility and wonder; their creations have certainly benefited mankind, and do indeed make our life more humane; neither are they forgetful of the debt owed to the great philosophers of the past or present, and in no way think their own thoughts to be final or more "progressive;" it would be impossible for them, even for a moment, to use the logic of scientific inquiry without remembering how Aristotle toiled to create Logic itself. No, that would be quite barbaric! Ah, but even here, Paolo, philosophy must stay true to its calling and remain ever vigilant. With one eye open, we must make sure that these well-intentioned ones do not fall into the error of "scientism" (what devotee of 'progress' would not be embarrassed by the bestial killing floor of our century and the connection between war and 'pure' science?) We should always remind them and ourselves (for technicians have now made their way into philosophy)[15] of what it means to be a "true beginner"— to look at things as if for the first time and see, with the innocence of a child, the world anew.

Science, being already well equipped with previous information and mathematical formulas, can and must plunge into the middle of things and immediately start taking them apart; if it did not do so—if it were to stop and reflect on its own activity, it would lose the practical advantage proper to it. But we students of philosophy,—we must always pause before the thing itself, and wonder what exactly constitutes the nature of "things in general," and further, how it is possible to know and have a world of things before our eyes, or that there is anything in being at all! We should maintain this state of self-imposed innocence and not be intimidated into silence by the grand achievements and sophistication of scientific methodology; rather, Paolo, we should

15. Here the Maestro is referring to the style of philosophy—analytic philosophy— which understands philosophical issues as only confusions of language and logic; for an extreme case, see *Language, Truth and Logic*, the positivism of A. J. Ayer

take courage and obstinately question the possibility, origin, and limits of such a method. By staying detached in this manner, philosophy will, of course, lose a certain kind of practical advantage, but will gain the "critical" advantage that most truly belongs to it. You see, every discipline or mode of inquiry must operate within the "region" which is appropriate to it; and each "region" calls for its own method, which in turn has its own results, limitations and dangers. Science belongs to the region of "natural phenomena" which means it requires a method that can handle all the various phenomena in physical space and time. And each of its particular sub-disciplines like biology, physics, and chemistry operate within their own sub-regions: if we do physics, for example, we must explore mass and energy in their quantifiable and external relations; if we do biology, our concern will be with forms of life in both their internal and adaptive and evolutionary changes; so each region or domain of objects will call for its own mode of inquiry—its own rules, parameters, and limitations. The region we choose to explore will in some sense dictate the best method and what kinds of information we find. In other words, Paolo, by looking at what by its nature is divisible and can be taken apart, we will, of course find what is quantifiable. It is by setting such specific limitations and rules on itself that science finds such exactness and fullness. If you select one corner of the house to clean, you will surely do a better job than if you were to attempt to clean the whole house, or a whole apartment building, or even a city block. What then, you ask, is the danger with such a pragmatically successful *modus operandi*? The danger, Paolo, lies right before our eyes! And that is that anything successful has a natural inclination to spread itself around—to try and obtain the same results, with the same method, wherever it can. Put another way, science is tempted by its success to measure everything in terms of its own corner of the world—that is, by the rules of divisibility and quantitative reasoning most appropriate to the domain of natural phenomena. Galileo and Descartes created a revolution when they applied mathematics to the world of extension. But the erroneous conclusion that has been drawn is that what doesn't fit or comply with this high standard of measurement and analysis—namely things from our life-world that require aesthetic, ethical or political judgment—is relegated to the realm of subjective opinion. In this way reason is thought of only as calculation, leaving the rest of our life world to the irrationality of opinion, relativism, and sophistry.[16]

The problem, Paolo, is that what works for one region may not necessarily work for another. We would certainly not want to reduce a work of art to one's neuronal connections or chemical interactions, nor would we consider love and human relations to be merely a matter of attraction and repulsion. While these concepts are quite useful for understanding things as a function of their material parts, science must be kept from the danger intrinsic to it of mistaking the "part" for the "whole"—the "tree" for the "forest." Just as with the "whole," the forest has a character of its own which cannot be equated with a single tree: imagine for a moment the sense of danger you experience when you venture forth from a well worn path into the depths of the forest: you will perhaps feel your heart beat a bit faster, and your forehead cool with moisture as the green canopy of trees closes in around you; your hearing will quickly attune itself to the strange sounds of crackling branches and creatures invisible to the eye; and as you carefully move, and listen to the silence between your foot falls, you will glimpse the fleeting shadows which leave only rustling leaves in their wake. All of this belongs to the mystery of the forest and cannot be explained by the nature of a tree.

Now, philosophy cannot possibly attain to the exactness that belongs to the examination of the 'part' or the closure and clarity obtained by the cleaning of one corner. It wants to sweep the whole house—nay, the whole city! And herein lies the danger

16. In short: relativism refers to the current pneumapathology of the psyche which seeks to reduce all nonscientific and practical-normative statements (ethical, political, aesthetic and religious...) to the biological level of the grunts and groans of subjective likes and dislikes: "that's your opinion," "who's to say," "that's your perception—your reality," and so forth. We have all but forgotten the realm or practical reason and the dialectical mode of inquiry, which is appropriate to the communication in the life-world.

intrinsic to philosophy. I mean, that because it desires to see the "whole;" it may become lost in the forest of speculation and unable to see the trees. Because philosophy is not primarily interested in the quantifiable analysis of the "part," it must often create new and, strange sounding forms of language—expressions that are needed for a thinking that contemplates the "whole;" and so, it cannot be limited by the exactness of mathematics nor the principles of experimental verification. Although the whole can be experienced, it cannot be verified nor discussed in the same way as its parts. But we must not confuse this lack of "exactness" with a lack of "rigor" in our thinking. Philosophy demands a different mode of thought—a thinking that puts into question all assumptions and so cannot rely on past findings nor accept traditional methodologies; it must always set out alone and start all over. It is the job of philosophy to avoid being bound by the rules and regulations of any "one" particular region of reality; its interest lies not so much in 'what' certain rules are, but rather 'how' rules in general are possible: are laws and formulas intrinsic to nature itself, or are they constructed by the mind? Can they be applied universally to what is both micro and macro in nature? Further, what do these different regions have in common, and what constitutes their difference? And most of all, what do these inquiries have to do with the good life, or why there is something in being rather than nothing?

You see, Paolo, what belongs to philosophy, as its own area of inquiry is nothing less than the "Region" of all particular regions—the "Ultimate Horizon" in which gods, men, beasts and things play out their destiny. So it must always be concerned with the possibility and connection of all things. And even if this cannot be known for sure,... even if we become impatient and fall into confusion,... even if we become temporarily lost in a world of abstractions—even so, we must never forsake our essential nature but take courage and endure the call to know.

Maestro

VARIATION SIX

On Philosophy and Education

Dear Paolo,

   I am doing well, and happy that you still think of your old friend, but as Alessandro has told you, I will soon be leaving for another place—hopefully, another orchard as beautiful as this one, with bountiful trees and perhaps some young workers with open hearts and curious minds. When I arrive, I will certainly inform you of my new location, and you, in turn, must continue to keep me apprised of your educational progress. In your last letter you mentioned the courses you are currently taking in order to complete the requirements necessary for your major field of study; but if you don't mind my saying so, Paolo, these are surely strange times when one is able to pursue such noble disciplines as science, law and medicine, or even become an engineer, or a teacher—be able, that is, to understand and practice these things with all but the slightest comprehension of the origin, genesis and general history of ideas which conditions and make possible each of these "particular" fields of study.

   We seem to be interested these days only in the immediate application and results of certain techniques and methods that yield useful effects. There seems to be no need for the more cumbersome "information" as to their historical development, or to their relation to larger problems. I suppose the success and proliferation of so many specialized areas of inquiry, where things can be produced that are easy to manipulate without much understanding of their origins, has made it easy for us to block out and barricade ourselves in our own subjective sensory shell. In short, our new modes of communication—radio, telephones, and TV—give us the simulation of being open to a larger world while in actuality staying within our own sensory membrane. In reality these tools which iconically represent the world produce a contracted being in the world and false sense of confidence. We are managing to live and learn in a world without knowing where we are or how we arrived at this particular historical destination using the tools and methods that we have. We live it seems, without proper location. But, ironically, what we need most in education, we do least. I mean, that nothing could be more timely than becoming 'situated'—especially now, when we modern men and women have suffered a triple displacement and radical dislocation ("radical," Paolo, should be read literally as being "rooted").

Just think Paolo, that at any other time in history one would wake up in the morning and feel themselves to be quite secure with where they were: they inhabited the earth which was situated at the center of the cosmos which was put there, no doubt, for their benefit. In the middle ages, people occupied a fixed place in a "Great Chain of Being" which stretched in descending degrees of being from Heaven to Hell below; and, even there, one would find levels and degrees of punishment. But now,... now things appear differently! We have since undergone three dislocations (what the Viennese Dr. Freud called "humiliations"): the first shock, initiated by Copernicus, was **Cosmological** in nature and concerned the discovery that the earth was not the center of creation; the second embarrassment is associated with Darwin's **Biological** deflation of man: that is, that we are not so special or different from our closest zoological relative—the ape; and the third humiliation is one claimed by Dr. Freud himself: to wit, that Reason—our **Psychological** crowning glory—sits capriciously upon a dark unexplained continent of irrational and unconscious drives.

I am afraid, Paolo, Copernicus unwittingly cast us like a particle of dust into the galactic winds of the Cosmo. We now find ourselves unmoored from our central position and left adrift in space, quite lost in what appears to be an explosion of infinite proportions. Even with the Newtonian Enlightenment the cosmos still appeared to be ordered like a clock designed by a transcendent craftsman. We thought, you see, if the cosmos was ordered, we could reliably count on human nature, social relations and laws to also be reasonably ordered—man is the "rational animal" in a rational universe! But now Paolo the rationality of the cosmos, if it can still be called that, lies at a much lower depth. The logos of the cosmos, as Heraclitus knew, remains profoundly unsounded. And if this cosmological shock weren't enough, Darwin came along and proceeded to point out what many others had become suspicious of for some time—a second dislocation and humiliation that showed an alternative explanation for the origin of life rather than the old top-down idea of creation: previously, the various forms of life could be neatly placed into forms and categories which preexist their material particulars; so each species could in essence remain eternally the same: a rose is always a plant, an ape is always an animal, and man was created just as he is—rational! But as you can surmise, this way of looking at things starts from the categories, or essences, first, then tries to find in a cursory fashion examples, which fit these categories. When we start with the actual observation of vital life, as Darwin did, we can see that it hardly fits such a precise, predetermined classification. Life rather shows itself as a sometimes discontinuous array of changing forms with varying degrees of gray between the black of 'this' and the white of 'that': we can observe plants that act like animals and fish which act like plants, and hundreds of other forms of life which defy simple and direct classification. When we say Homo Sapiens, for instance, do we mean to deny the obvious structural homology we share with transitional creatures on the Serengeti Planes? Nietzsche, rather thought of the ape as a "painful embarrassment," and that man was "closer to the ape than to Plato." [Since this was written, the analysis of our genes shows that we are related to Neanderthals; ed.] The point is, Paolo, that we have been both "Cosmologically" and "Biologically" dislocated from our homocentric position. Are we, perhaps, not the being to end all beings, but a slightly comical transitional figure on the way to something beyond ourselves? And what of our claim to being· the "rational animal"? What if this claim upon which we have placed so much of our dignity, is nothing but a ruse and a mask, which hides a deeper and more insidious drive for power and procreation? If Schopenhauer, Nietzsche, and Freud are right, we cannot for a moment look at ourselves the same way—not, that is, without keeping a straight face! This last "Psychological" humiliation completes the triple dislocation of man from his former privileged position. And yet, we go about our daily business as though nothing has happened.

That is why I say, Paolo, that nothing could be timelier than for education to once again take up its task and give up the mentality of the market place where courses are bartered and sold to curious window shoppers. Educators must give up their roles as shopkeepers, headcounters and corner-sweepers—give these up and reassert their proper responsibility as leaders. Let us beckon them from the *agora* and welcome them back to the academy. It is no mere coincidence that the word "educate" derives its meaning from the verb "to lead" (educere); and to lead means, among other things, to call one forth and show the way, that is, to bring one from one place to another location—to lead one out of the corner, as it were, and into the clearing. And what, dear Paolo, is this clearing? It is a place of rest and relocation—a "well-lit place" in the middle of an always-encroaching darkness. The clearing is a prepared place which allows us time and security to regroup our forces and get a better view of our situation; for it is only when the foliage of the jungle has been cut back that the cultural life of man can begin to flourish and grow; it is in the light of the clearing that civilization is able to sustain itself, and it does so through its cultural activities—through the use of tools, art and ideas about "where" one is, "what" one is, and "why" one should do this or that! And each of us, Paolo, like each generation, has its own way of dwelling in the clearing—its own way, that is, of coming to grips with its historical situation and particular location. This is what we mean by the cultural life of our species, that is, that culture is a way of reflecting on, and expressing the joys and sorrows of one's location; so we can say provisionally that to educate is to "lead" one into one's proper cultural location—to show how one is doing and dwelling in ones given historical clearing.

Now all this, of course, presupposes that the teacher, as leader and guide, has attempted to make his/her way through the labyrinth of man's historical-cultural existence and can, therefore, show the way into the clearing. But alas, what we find on all levels are not guides but well-intentioned blind men and women leading the blind into the false security of the market place and further into the barbarism of specialization and monetary exchange. Let's be quite honest about the present situation: I mean, to merely teach one "how" to do something—to give one special technique or method without properly locating him/her—why, this is both foolish and dangerous! Can you imagine, Paolo, arriving at some place without knowing how you got there, where you came from, or what you ought to do with yourself? Then, Paolo, imagine being taught how to build a fire and use a weapon. These tools and techniques will undoubtedly help you get through the night, but will not be sufficient to hold back the force of the jungle and preserve the space of civilization. This is done with the help of a different kind of tool. What a leader as educator must do is assist us in situating ourselves by tracing our way back and showing how our past location is related to our present one. He or she must brave the journey backwards in order to locate us and lead us forward without ending up once again at our point of departure. But, unfortunately, educators have abrogated the responsibility of "leading" and "locating" and have themselves been lead into the agora where they have succumbed to a plethora of delightful colors, smells, and the sounds of hawkers. Forgetful of "leading" and "locating", they have been put to sleep by a myth most common to "buying" and "selling."

The myth, about which I speak—which by the way, has become quite potent, persistent and pervasive in its soporific power—is what I would call the "Myth of Spontaneous Combustion." What is referred to by this term is the complete lack of historical sense concerning all things bought and sold: in matters of business, each situation, product, or rate of exchange is considered as though it popped here out of nowhere; yesterday's monetary values are discarded, and each day—nay, each hour brings with it a new situation disconnected and irrelevant to the last. [Today, with access to instantaneous communication, stocks are traded in terms of milliseconds.] What is important is that which is in "demand" now! If there is no demand, there is no value. This leads to the first equation of the market place—(value = demand). And if this is the first axiom of the market place, then what follows naturally as a corollary is the idea that the "new" thing in demand is more valuable than the old. The second equation is, therefore—(new = better). The logic of the market place dictates that something old be discarded; after all, if we were content to stay with the old, there would be no material improvement, profit or work,... the shops would all close! So, as you can see, these equations are necessary for the bartering of commodities, but fundamentally in error when applied to education. If we consider what is old as useless junk, then one of the great entrepreneurs of the time is right when he says "history is bunk" [ed. attributed to Henry Ford].

When education is viewed from the perspective of the "free market" and the criterion of success is measured in terms of a business model, the past will be understood as a sordid affair of material deprivation and obsolete ideas; and in concurrence, the future is seen as a place where the new and better—as the smaller, bigger, faster—awaits us. Ideas, like old products, will be relegated to the archaic junk heap of the past. The student under commercialized pedagogy will, like everyone else, be understood as a consumer; and a teacher will be one who facilitates a skill or provides a service for his or her shoppers. The ideas being sold are like commodities to the student/consumer; and in accordance with this vicious business dialectic, the student, in turn, becomes a commodity in terms of the administrative regime. What was the teacher now becomes the sales manager who provides double entry accounting procedures and data retrieval concerning the numerical growth and "success" of his/her department [store]. If seen this way, what becomes important for educators is to show "how" we can take advantage of, understand and use the latest products and techniques; it becomes important for them to create a new kind of consumer and at the same time create a work force to supply the latest demands. In that way, education stays in business! But should we treat persons as commodities—as objects of exchange that are subject to the laws of supply and demand? We can, of course, and do, consider people from an objective and statistical point of view: when, with a medical procedure, for instance, a doctor temporarily looks upon one as an object of analysis in order to restore one's health. But to do this as an everyday practice would degrade one's being to the level of a thing. But we are a being that is thrown open to the future—a possible being—and, therefore, cannot be reduced to a thing until death. The data driven business model, which has now infiltrated the academy, treats students as consumers and places all relations under the rubric of supply and demand.

Of course, there are currently many courses in the Humanities and Sciences that explore nature and the human condition,—there is no end to the subdivisions and quantity of information being disseminated! But these facts, remembered events, and parcels of information are often studied as though they had no basis in the history of ideas—no qualitative milieu. Facts and remembered events cannot be fully understood without seeing the larger background of ideas, metaphysical assumptions, and types of discourse which make them possible or relevant. Every object of study, like every object in nature, always exists within, and presupposes a more comprehensive horizon. [Today in the philosophy of science one would say that every fact is "theory laden" ed.] As you have heard me say many times Paolo, part of every individual thing, which is, is also constituted by its surroundings. Nothing spontaneously pops up out of nowhere, especially not the human mind and its ideas.[17] Part of what we are is to be found in the dark recesses of our biological past; and part of what we are can be understood in terms of our past individual psychology; but more importantly, who we are and how we understand ourselves and others is always dependent upon a larger philosophical-historical picture—what we can call our 'vital

---

17. Coming from Europe in the early part of the 20th century, the Maestro is obviously aware of Heidegger's term for human awareness "Dasein" or being there. We do not find ourselves as an "I" locked up in our heads, but as a temporal field of being already in a world of meaning and history. For Heidegger, Dasein is thrown into the world; we do not merely 'have' a history, but 'are' historical in our being.

location'. This, Paolo, is the place within which we decide on "matters of importance" and the beliefs for which we will stake our lives.

We are individuals submersed in a historical-cultural life made up of ideas about what we value, believe, or think we 'ought' to do; and these norms and imperatives, Paolo, are counterfactual and cannot be reduced to what 'is' the case, but what 'ought' to be. So it is the job of philosophy to always be vigilant, always aware of the concepts, ideas, and contradictions in play around and below our ordinary opinions and practices... before they do their mischief. And in respect to those of the past who no longer have a voice, we should remember that the opening of Western civilization— whatever its results and predicaments—begins when the **"philosopher"**—the lover of wisdom—takes a courageous stand against the **"philodoxer,"** as the lover of opinion. This stand, now forgotten and occluded by technology, is the incipient moment and founding event of universal education. And this means that all humans are beings who are open to the truth of Being; and as such—they can fall into errancy and deceit. No animal can lie, Paolo, simply because no animal bears the burden of being the site where the disclosure or covering over of Being takes place.

But modern education no longer takes as its model the "care of the soul" as the site of disclosure, but rather mimics the ways of business and the operations of the machine. In this way the tension and *agon* of the psyche is pacified and the valorization of wisdom over opinion is reversed. There is no greater proof of this, Paolo, then the erasure and cancellation of the word "philodoxer." When we erase the antagonistic symbol, we destroy the protagonist and hero of the quest for universal education. But in face of the wondrous products and applications of science, education has handed over the search for truth to the operational 'know how' of technology. The false conclusion which follows is that what doesn't submit to 'quantitative' analysis, that is, what cannot be reduced to causal and statistical relations, is relegated to subjective opinion and its consequent relativism. Socrates knew that this kind of subjective empowerment and control could create a tyrannical psyche, which would inevitably find its way into the policies and cacophony of the crowd. I'm afraid Paolo, that teachers have unwittingly taken the side of their historical enemies—the sophists: they now encourage students to communicate in ways that please the crowd, score points in a debate, use effective talking points, say only what's popular or politically correct, and as Socrates said about the sophist: "they make the better seem the worst, and the worst seem the better!"

What then is to be done? We can invite our educators to put aside the latest methodologies and initiate what Vico called a Recorsi: that is, to commence with a return to the incipient moment of our educational tradition. If we do this we will experience and understand that "philosophy" is not merely a "worldview," or another interesting "opinion;"... nor is it one more subject for the curious to investigate—as though, Paolo, we were once again shopping! We will find that the general and fundamental questions which philosophy deals with await every particular area of inquiry,... when that inquiry or discipline faces a crisis in its foundations and assumptions: when, for instance, the mathematician faces a paradox, or asks what a number 'is'; or when physics asks about the nature of matter; or biology questions the essence of life,... and so on. Philosophy is not a course that one may choose to take or not to take, but a level of discourse, which belongs to all human beings—all too often when they hit bottom! But most importantly, Paolo, if we commence with a return to the incipient moment of what we call education, we will see that the symbol "Philosopher" stands for a certain *pathos* and affliction of the psyche—a psyche which has been struck and shaken by Being and the inexhaustible pursuit of truth. If we do this we will once again experience the birth of education out of the spirit of philosophy.

III

FAREWELL ADDRESS

Concerning One's True Home

"To dwell, to be set at peace, means to remain at peace within the free, the preserve, the free sphere that safeguards each thing in its nature."
- Heidegger

I am deeply moved that so many of you have come here tonight for the last of our meetings together, but saddened that I, like some of you, must leave my homeland for distant and foreign shores. It is surely the highest of ironies that we must meet here in secret—an irony of global proportions that all but the most superficial of ideas have been banned from discussion precisely at this moment in time when great Ideologies stand hovering over the earth like giant specters poised for battle. How peculiar it is that when man finds a particular philosophy to suit his needs, he quickly disposes of the need for philosophy; then just as quickly does he proceed to ensconce himself behind this philosophy declaring all other views dangerous and untrue. But as we have learned, both from history and our own personal lives, the crowning of one view as the sole truth is the deathblow to the philosophical life. You know by now, dear students, that a particular philosophy is merely a glimpse of the truth—a way station and resting place along the way which can never constitute or be confused with the "spirit of philosophy."[18]

Before I depart, however, I think it appropriate and timely that we discuss the phenomenon of being-at-home: our home is usually considered the place where we are best centered—a place where our position is well defined within the boundaries of family, tradition and physical space. It is both a place from which we can safely depart and project ourselves outward and into the future, and also a place of refuge to return to and find respite from the ceaseless assault of the other. At home we find our comfort and happiness in being where we belong, and being with what in turn belongs to us. Our happiness, then, has much to do with being and dwelling where we belong, and being where we belong means to be-at-home.

18. This talk—placed last for aesthetic purposes—is chronologically first and comes before Maestro's arrival in America. He is concerned in the first paragraph with the growing misuse and occlusion of the term 'philosophy': it has come to be identified, almost exclusively, with a 'world view', or the holding of any belief or opinion; but in historical actuality, philosophy refers to a constant dialectical movement between 'holding' and 'doing', that is, with the constant analysis and critique of a belief or opinion.

The curious thing is that we are never fully aware of being-at-home until this fragile structure of belonging has been fractured—until, that is, we experience the anxiety of homelessness. We all know there are moments when the peace of our home degenerates into the alien space of a house, or times when the unity of our family is ruptured and the rituals of tradition broken. During these times of displacement, a gnawing feeling tells us that something is not right with our world—that we do not belong. And so we move on to a different house, or town, or job, find different people to be with, or perhaps, change our traditional beliefs. But we all know that it will be only a matter of time until we once again hear the silent whisper of discontent that beckons us on to other things. Let us learn once and for all, my students, that this disturbance is a terminal condition of the human spirit! We are not beings whose essential nature is to be found in being-at-home and self-satisfied; but rather, it is because we are first of all displaced and homeless that we can yearn so strongly for happiness and home.[19]

How bleak, you are thinking, is a philosophy that considers man's condition as essentially homeless, and so renders him incapable of happiness. Not so! The question is whether one attempts to gain happiness born of a forgetfulness which leads from one temporary shelter to another, or a happiness found in remembering and being thoughtful of that to which we always belong: when we are forgetful, or distracted, we are caught up in the rhythm and flow of the things around us and begin to think we belong to a job, place, house, role, or even to a means of transportation or products of communication. But we are not things! We are not merely one kind of a thing—a subject—manipulating the objects around us; we are, rather a way of "being toward the world" [This, of course, is a reference to Heidegger's term in Being in Time—ed.]; and this 'way' that the worldly context and meaning of the things we use lights up for us is not a

19. Maestro is, once again, using Heidegger's analysis of 'mood', that is, that before cognitive and reflective thinking, Dasein is 'attuned' in a certain way to the world. Anxiety reveals what Heidegger calls unheimlich—a feeling of being 'estranged'.

thing itself. This being 'not' a thing introduces into our being a feeling of emptiness, which we endlessly try to fill. But some dissatisfaction will always haunt the multiple diversions of life. Only Gods and animals can enjoy the happiness of being immediate and in the moment. But this feeling of happiness should really be called 'satisfaction'. Why? Because if a thing is totally at home with itself, it could not really know the happiness of being-at-home; for this, as we can surmise, is only revealed through the ever present possibility of self-displacement and reflection. Although the gods have blessed us with the fruit of forgetfulness and other sweet diversions, we must not stay too long in the house of oblivion. Our happiness must be found in the place where we most truly belong. But where is this place—and what would this other kind of happiness be like?

Before I suggest an answer—one which must always remain tentative and questionable—we should listen once again to what is being said in Plato's Allegory of the Cave. Let us imagine, for a moment, that we are like cave dwellers who from the time of our birth have been chained and shackled to one position in the cave. We would, for the most part, be quite content to eat, sleep and be amused by the playful shadowgraphs and simulacra that dance across the only wall we can see. As in the cinema theater we are lost in the representations of the world and feel secure for a while within the frame of a false cavernous horizon. But suppose, then, that there is one among us, a rebel of sorts, who grows discontent and suspects that there is life beyond the cave; so, he struggles to break his chains and turns around towards the stream of light coming from the opening of the cave; but as he turns toward the light, his eyes squint shut and he begins to fall. You can imagine how foolish he begins to look to his fellow cave dwellers: "where is he going!" they cry. A clamor will rise from the crowd concerning his sanity: "why, he who leaves this happy place is surely mad!" But there is something deep inside our friend that urges him toward the light. And so he makes his way to the opening where he finally stands in the blinding light of day. What he sees, as his eyes slowly adjust, is another dimension where people go about their daily business of bartering and carrying objects. He is, no doubt, confused by all this and tempted to run back to the world he knew—back to his home. But the longer he stays out, the easier it becomes to see and sort things out. He now sees that the shadows below are merely reflections of objects that have their source in the light of the sun above. At this point our friend must endure a moment of truth. To which world does he belong? Should he stay or should he go back? If he stays, what he gains in clarity of mind he will lose in familiarity—in home, family and friends; if he goes back, he will look like an uncommonsensical and impractical fool. As you know, in Plato's story our friend takes up his mission of clarity and returns to tell his fellow cave dwellers of this different world.

Now, if you will allow me to take some liberty with the moral of Plato's story: I would like to suggest that happiness, like the quest for knowledge, is also constituted by certain essential moments; the first moment is grounded in the desire for **security.** In this frame of mind we are happy to live and look at things in the accustomed manner—a manner that keeps us safely within the repetitious cycle and encompassing of our traditional beliefs. This first kind of happiness is, of course, predicated on how much we refuse to see, or how much we are unable to see. Unaware of the limitations of our cave, we remain quite comfortable with our shadows and simulacra; there we stay, lodged in a state of willing belief and child-like ignorance—an innocent ignorance that can have mischievous consequences of its own.

The second moment of happiness is initiated by the will to **freedom,** which manifests itself in a feeling of discontent and a subsequent desire to escape what we now see as the confines of the enclosure and the opinions of the theater crowd. We see that we have merely inherited our cave and its shadows, and that it is, perhaps, only a part of a larger situation. And so we leave our state of child-like innocence in pursuit of what truly belongs to us—we leave for the world of freedom and experience. We think we will find where we belong by doing many things; we will weigh and test and find what makes us happy. The danger at this juncture is that we may become suspended in the twilight of ambiguity in perpetual pursuit of what makes us happy—neither able to go back to our cave, nor forward and into the light of the clearing. As you know, we can experience many places and things and be none the wiser.

So, the third moment in the quest for happiness involves the love of **truth**. This desire is not to be confused with the concupiscential desires of the cave, but is often born of despair. It is a movement of the psyche toward self-reflection, which happens when the unhappy and forgetful consciousness, which lay dormant but ever present in the previous stages of happiness, becomes fully aware of itself. I say unhappy, for with the light of day will necessarily come the revelation of our true situation—and our true situation, dear students, is that we are displaced and cannot be fully situated. Like our fellow prisoners from Plato's cave who cannot stay too long in the sun, nor endure its blinding light, we too must return to our cave knowing that we belong to neither place. Sadly, we see that we are neither finite cave dwelling creatures nor infinitely enlightened Gods. To what, then, do we belong? And how will we ever overcome the melancholy of homelessness?

What we have been looking for—what seemed so far away—has all along been close at hand. If we are not beasts nor gods, not able to live in darkness nor in light, both a thing and a reflection on a thing, neither body nor mind alone, neither able to live in a cave nor out, then it is precisely this "difference" which constitutes our essential being. If we are a being who dwells in "difference" then we do not belong to "this" nor "that", but to the hinterland of neither place—to the open and free region which draws us forth and shelters us in its clearing as beings who are "open", "free", and "in-between." And so we will not find authentic happiness—a happiness which does not hide its inner despair—until we commence with the fourth and final movement: the will to **return** to that which we already are, in the place we have been all along. We will return to that from which there is no escape. Upon our return, however, we will dwell with the things around us, not in our former state of ignorance and self-deceit, but in a state of philosophical suspension—an ignorance that is aware of itself and all that still remains to be thought beyond the false horizon that surrounds and makes possible the cave of our existence. The happiness gained by this return is not the kind which is had in stolen moments of forgetfulness, but is one which is grounded in a thinking which stays mindful and remembers our essential being as beings who are open to the openness of Being. To think philosophically is to be concerned with, and, therefore, grateful of the gift of Being. Although we must return to the finite boundaries of our environment, we will do so knowing that our nature is not completely defined in darkness by the cave walls which surround us, but is also claimed by the light of Being. So by remembering the mystery of that which withdraws from our grasp and so forever remains to be thought, we will stay close to what is the true home and refuge of our being—close to, and sheltered in the sanctuary of Being's clearing.

Do not be concerned, then, by my departure from our homeland, nor dismayed at my movement from one place to another, for I will keep you in my heart and remain steadfast in my resolve. Remember, my leaving is also my gift to you—a gift of love that allows you a place to come forth. Farewell, then, and take notice that the difference between the first kind of happiness and the last—the happiness born of oblivion and the happiness found in thoughtful recollection—the difference, as you can see, often resides in a tear.

EPILOGUE

At about the same time the foregoing documents were found, another crime against philosophy was being committed in Prague: this time against the Czechoslavakian philosopher Jan Patočka. He was interrogated for over eleven hours and succumbed to a massive brain hemorrhage, most likely for being a signatory of Charta 77:

> *"All it did was to remind the government that the ideals of human dignity and civic freedom which it had itself promulgated in its laws and in the international agreements it signed were being routinely violated in practice, and to call on the society as whole to support the government in making sure that the rule of law shall prevail over arbitrary misuse of power"*[20]

As with Socrates, Patočka came forth in a time of need and forgetfulness and took a stand between the oppressor and oppressed—the city-state (polis) and the soul—and spoke for those who were silenced by power, popular opinion (doxa) and death. Philosophy—if one is to be in fidelity to its emergence and incipient moment—reminds us that political injustice (macrocosm) has its motivating force in the dynamics of the individual psyche (microcosm) and what it is drawn by and directed toward (intentionality). This internal examination is crucial for the 'liberated' psyche of democracy, which often seeks freedom without limits. But we know empirically, and at first hand, that the psyche, if led by its consuming appetites and aggressive passions—by what St. Augustine calls the 'libido domanandi'—is subject to becoming addicted and tyrannical. (The soul should not be understood, here, as an entity, but rather as an emergent property, which awakens from its prereflective and preindividuated animal state of immediacy and begins to directly experience itself as an agonal 'tension' between (metaxy) oppositional

---

[20] Erazim Kohk, Jan Patočka, *Philosophy and Selected Writings* (University of Chicago Press, Chicago and London, 1989) p.3

forces. The human soul is born as an imperative to know and order itself—to care!)

The soul which remains diffuse and out of order (adikia, unjust) will simply transfer this confusion into the social-political domain of the larger self where it is easily seduced and attracted to what it likes and dislikes; it will seek the approval of the 'they'—and what 'they' say: and what 'they' say, by definition, can only be an opinion and semblance of the truth and does not reflect the more difficult decision to engage in an individual process of self disclosure. The mob, like the disordered soul, is not capable of taking responsibility for itself and what it believes. The philosophically deprived soul—the soul without a beautiful and welcoming city and the support of loving friends (philia) to help direct its eros and energy to the good—will fall into the crowd and its simulacra and simulation. And, as Kierkegaard also warned: "where the crowd goes, there goes the untruth." But even more dangerously—and as history sadly shows—the crowd may seek out a scapegoat for their own disorder, and in their rampage and contagion require a human sacrifice.

From Patočka's own words, we hope to show an agreement with the writings presented here on the spirit of philosophy:

> "Care of the soul is that which Socrates does, constantly examining our opinions about what is good. Each of our acts, each of our thoughts and each our deed is in the formal sense aiming for something, for some kind of goal. This goal such, in its formal guise, we call the good. Examining what is good is care of the soul. We examine also in order to keep that of which we have once had insight."[21]

---

[21]   Jan Patočka, *Plato and Europe* (Stanford University Press, Stanford CA. 2002) p.120

Made in the USA
Las Vegas, NV
05 September 2023

77123962R00090